# PRAISE FOR WIDOW'S MOON

"*Widow's Moon* comes to us as a guiding light of hope, resilience, and the power of the human heart to heal and transform in the face of unimaginable tragedy. Through the pages of this heart-opening, vulnerable, and exquisitely written book you will see yourself and know that you are not alone in your journey of grief. Regardless of what kind of loss you have been through, you will benefit from Hope's wise and loving teachings—everything we go through in life is a teacher for us and here to support our spiritual growth. This is most certainly the message of our times! I truly can't recommend this book enough, and I offer a deep bow of gratitude for this inspirational, authentic sharing of one courageous woman's pathway through loss and how our grief can serve as a powerful catalyst for spiritual growth and transformation. Hope is a beautiful person with a big heart, who took the time to confront and move through her grief and now this book is here for all to benefit from her profound healing journey."

**—Wendy Black Stern**,
C-IAYT, founder of the *Grief Support Network, Inc.*
Owner of the *Center for Somatic Grieving, LLC*

"*Widow's Moon* is a wise and compassionate exploration of love, loss, and transformation. This book will be a gift to many. If you're feeling alone, confused, and unsupported—as so many of us do while grieving—allow this book to companion you through your own loss."

**—Tanja Pajevic,**
author of *The Secret Life of Grief*

"Amid the pain and grief of unexpected death, there arises a roller coaster of overwhelming emotions that creep into the psyche at the most unexpected hours of daytime or nighttime. *Widow's Moon* is a superb personal account of loss, grief, spirit messages, the journey back to life, and finally accepting life amongst the living again. It is an astounding account of how the deepest grief can be the catalyst to a spiritually guided journey back to the living at just the right time. I highly recommend it."

**—Janet D. Tarantino,**
author of *Dying to See: Revelations About God,*
*Jesus, Our Pathways, and The Nature of the Soul*

"Cara Hope's *Widow's Moon* is a beautiful and heart-wrenching story of losing her dear husband to suicide and how she had to navigate the chaos of immense grief. She brings you along both her inner and outer process and gives you an intimate look into what helped her come out the other side stronger. She's truly a grief warrior. She gives you many practical tools to help you with your own grief journey with whatever loss you may be experiencing. I found it similar to my own journey to befriend grief after losing my partner to quadriplegia. We need more books on our intimate experiences of grief like this one! Thank you Hope for giving us all HOPE!"

**—Beth Erlander,** MA, LPC, ATR,
grief friend, psychotherapist & grief support practitioner

"Cara Hope Clark is a master storyteller and brave truth-teller. In *Widow's Moon*, she lets us into the harrowing journey of losing her husband to suicide with grace, skill, and heart. Never self-indulgent, always with an eye to transformation. If you've ever lost anyone to suicide, read this book. And if you've ever lost anyone at all, the themes she touches on are so universal, it's relevant for all of us."

—**Johanna Walker**, TEDx speaker

"Cara's journey through grief is a reminder that the practice of rituals can help each of us find the treasures hidden in the darkness. *Widow's Moon* is a precious gift to all those who are dancing with grief."

—**Kitty Edwards**,
Executive Director, The Living &
Dying Consciously Project

"*Widow's Moon* is a deep, honest, intimate journey through the masterful teachings of Grief. Cara Hope takes us with her through all the layers of her metamorphic journey to the ultimate emergence into love and acceptance. Full of wisdom, guidance, and hope, this medicine story offers much to anyone who is experiencing grief. If you are ready for the alchemy of your own journey, I highly recommend *Widow's Moon* as a guide, teacher, and friend."

—**Marianne Lindstrom Mitchell**,
energy healer, spiritual counselor

"I am impressed with Cara's ability to write about such a difficult period of her life. Her story unfolds in a truly compelling and engaging way, and her voice is authentic and relatable. Within the story, she weaves her insights and wisdom with practical suggestions and guidance. Whether you are new to the journey of grief or it's a road well-traveled, you will find this book deeply moving and inspirational"

—**Eeris Kallil**, *LMT CLT*

"*Widow's Moon* is a beacon of light that shines for those navigating the turbulent seas of grief. Cara Hope's story creates a vessel of healing through deeply honoring the ever-changing cycles of grief while holding a higher awareness of purpose and meaning. Her generous and applicable tools are alchemical gold for those who have sustained heartbreaking loss and are on their own journey toward health and wholeness. Thank you for your courage and wisdom, Cara Hope!"

—**Lisa Schiavone**,
healer, teacher, evolutionary astrologer

"A beautiful and raw rendition of the heroine's journey, Cara eloquently shares with us how she turned loss and grief into Hope. Moving. Inspiring."

—**Dr. Skye Zimmermann**,
transformational coach

"*Widow's Moon* is an honest and inspiring memoir. This story takes us through Hope's journey to reclaim her connection to Source, and to what it means to live life fully again. It is a heart-wrenching yet poignant account of how she found the courage to face the days and years that followed her husband's suicide. Immensely readable and full of guidance and encouragement …one brave woman's journey back to life."

—**Lisa Bluedeer**,
spiritual intuitive, shamanic practitioner

"If you are looking for inspiration, *Widow's Moon* is for you. It's one of those books that just flows and you can't stop reading it. It definitely motivates you to do your part to move through the grief life can sometimes place upon us. I found *Widow's Moon* to be incredibly powerful and am so grateful to Cara Hope for having the guts to write it."

—**Gwen Cupples**, midwife of awakening

"*Widow's Moon* is an exceptionally well-written story about overcoming grief. A comprehensive toolbox of suggestions and multiple resources is generously sprinkled throughout this book of compassion and understanding. The author eloquently shares her grief that occurs when her husband passes from suicide, yet this book is appropriate for anyone who is experiencing any form of suffering. She shares her journey with clarity, optimism, and strength. She explains multiple healing modalities used to help process and overcome this event while she moves forward.

This eloquent story is filled with empowering self-love concepts and beautiful imagery appropriate for all readers. Cara Hope Clark's courage is stunning and provides strength to readers looking to find support for their journey. Much wisdom is shared in an exquisite voyage through grief. Beautiful symbolic analogies are presented in this carefully crafted and beautifully paced book. *Widow's Moon* is highly recommended for anyone in any stage of grief that would appreciate receiving multiple avenues of resolution."

—**Rebecca Austill-Clausen**,
award-winning author of *Change Maker:
How My Brother's Death Woke Up My Life*

"*Widow's Moon* is an inspiring, true story that assures us that we can and will survive devastating losses in our lives. Hope exposes her most vulnerable self in sharing her arduous journey following the unexpected suicide of her loving husband, Claude. From the moment of his passing, as she finds her way through the hilly countryside of her grief, there are moments of top-of-the-mountain clarity and sunshine, and moments of deep, rocky ravines that leave her wondering how she will possibly build her new life.

In this riveting memoir, we live and breathe the shock and pain of loss and the triumphs of the tiniest steps back to wholeness. Hope shares her deep learning along the journey, lessons to us all that support surrounds us and will light our way.

The gift to all who read this spellbinding memoir is an understanding of the unpredictability of grief – of how we can try to bring it to an end as quickly as possible, yet it will take all the time it needs. There are great insights for supporting others in their grief."

**—Risë Severson Kasmirski,**
#1 bestselling author of *When Paradise Speaks,*
*A remarkable, true story of friendship,*
*after-death communication, and art that heals*

"*Widow's Moon* expresses the essence of the season of grief from losing a life partner to suicide. It demonstrates the courage, fortitude, and wisdom of the surviving spouse's spiritual journey in pure authenticity."

**—Jennifer Angelee,**
teacher, healer, and bestselling author of *Beloved,*
*I Can Show You Heaven*

# Widow's Moon

# Widow's Moon

## A Memoir of Healing, Hope & Self-Discovery Through Grief & Loss

## CARA HOPE CLARK

WIDOW'S MOON
A Memoir of Healing, Hope & Self-Discovery Through Grief & Loss

Editor: Rebecca van Laer
Proofreader: Susan Nunn
Cover Designer: Pagatana Design Service—pagatana.com
Illustrators: Tatyana Matsiushkova & Aya Lormus
Book Interior and E-book Designer: Amit Dey—amitdey2528@gmail.com
Author's photo: Steve Gaudin—stevegaudinphotography.com
Production & Publishing Consultant: Geoff Affleck—geoffaffleck.com

ISBN: 978-1-7371414-0-2 (Paperback)
ISBN: 978-1-7371414-1-9 (eBook)

Library of Congress Number: 2021908685

BIO026000 BIOGRAPHY & AUTOBIOGRAPHY / Personal Memoirs
SEL010000 SELF-HELP / Death, Grief, Bereavement
PSY037000 PSYCHOLOGY / Suicide

# DOWNLOAD YOUR
# SUPPORTIVE GIFTS

D iscovering empowering practices after the loss of your loved one can be an important step on your healing and transformational path through grief. With my *Sacred Shrines & Altars* guide and *Printable Affirmations Cards*, you will discover methods for creating your own personal rituals and explore ways to tend and care for yourself as you grieve.

Your gift includes:

1. *Widow's Moon* **Sacred Shrines and Grief Altars** *(Audio Guide & PDF instructions)*
2. *Widow's Moon* **Printable Affirmation Cards**

Choose to honor your path through grief by downloading your free gifts today at widowsmoon.com/gifts.

# DEDICATION

To Claude, my beloved husband, who descended
into darkness, so that others may ascend
into the light.

To Noah, our dear son who has embraced his life with
dedication and commitment in the face of adversity,
always striving to live in a way that would
make his father proud.

# TABLE OF CONTENTS

# INTRODUCTION

During a session with my massage therapist, and deep in a meditative state, I heard a clear communication from my angelic guides: *Don't let the idea that you are small keep you from believing that you can make a difference.*

Internalizing this pronouncement was one of the many things that empowered me to convey these words to you. If you had told me years ago that I would one day write a memoir about the most intimate and painful experience of my life—my husband Claude's suicide—I would have laughed in your face. I never had any aspirations of being an author. Of course, I also never expected to lose my husband before his time. Yet here I am, having survived what was previously unimaginable. Here I am, answering the call of my soul. That guidance has stretched me in ways I could never have foreseen, pulling me along for the ride of my life!

It has been a long journey from the sudden catastrophe of untold loss to the process of completing a book. Grief is one of the most primal emotions for us to experience as humans. When we lose someone who is an integral part of our lives, the space that is left can feel like a gaping wound that will never heal, much less reform to create something new. From the vantage point of utter devastation, we are engulfed in shock, sadness, and disbelief. We wonder how we could possibly see our way through this. As a result, some spend months, years, or even decades in this frozen wasteland of despair.

It's important to honor and respect all aspects and timelines of our grief, giving it room to evolve on its own schedule. Grief can be a roaring lion, a faint memory, and everything in between. No one can truly say how it will or should look for someone else.

Yet there are certain categories of grief. For instance, to be a 'widow' or 'widower' is different than to lose a parent. I have discovered that when we lose a life partner, we feel left alone and adrift in our sorrow. After all, we have lost our 'other half,' the person we had built our life around and devoted ourselves to. We are left alone in silence, only to ask ourselves, *Who am I, standing here now without my beloved by my side?*

I imagine that my story as a widow may be easily relatable to others who have suffered the loss of their spouse. If you share this experience, I'd like to invite you to reframe the way you regard the word 'widow' or 'widower.' In our culture, this label can carry a negative connotation involving how we view our identity. Taking on the mantle of the widow was one of the last things that I would have wanted to experience as a woman. However, being a widow (or widower) does not have to mean we are dried up, hopeless, and lifeless, ever descending into a life of misery. Our lives don't have to end when our other halves' do. Quite the opposite. Over these many years since Claude's suicide, I have elevated the word 'widow.' I now see it as a badge of courage, signaling entrance onto a sacred evolutionary path.

Though this book is written from a widow's perspective, my journey has imparted lessons that I feel can be helpful to all those who grieve. These include learning how to hold space for grief, honoring and caring for oneself through grief, and within the midst of it all, loving and embracing one's perfectly imperfect self.

Although the loss of those you love is devastating beyond measure, it can also serve to crack you wide open in ways you never could have imagined. With your higher wisdom guiding you, you have the unexpected opportunity to reflect on your identity and the life narrative you were participating in. This season of grief holds the potential of awakening and claiming new aspects of yourself that were previously dormant or yet undiscovered.

Some Native American tribes associate distinctive seasonal or energetic characteristics with the moon, leading to the symbolic naming of each full moon—for example, the Growing Moon or Pink Moon in April carries with it the energy of rebirth, renewal, and the re-emergence of the varied pink wildflowers.

*Widow's Moon* embraces this tradition. This moon phase honors the divine feminine. In addition, it encompasses a potent invitation, asking us to harness the power of grief as a catalyst for awakening, growth, and transformation. It carries the full potentiality to redefine who we are and who we have come to be in this present incarnation.

Prior to Claude's death, I grew up believing that all of our earthly experiences serve a higher purpose. This understanding had already supported my ever-maturing development of faith and trust. Thankfully, with this spiritual belief in place, I had the courage and inner resources I needed to process my loss.

I have my mom to thank for laying the foundational belief system that I have built upon in adulthood. When I was a child, she taught me that "All things happen as part of a divine plan" and that "God helps those who help themselves."

From my vantage point as a woman who has been through many painful events, I can see that she was coming from a purely transcendent perspective. I never once saw her fall into the trap of feeling sorry for herself. Despite her lifelong struggle with chronic physical pain, she never saw herself as a victim. It was quite the opposite. She was unbending in her resolve to find the silver lining woven into her life struggles. Oftentimes, she would say that many were worse off than she was. She focused on cultivating gratitude for the blessings she did have. Again and again, I wondered how she had the strength to hold that position considering how much she endured on a daily basis.

As a child, seeing her move through life with this determination despite her illness informed my adult life in far-reaching ways. She taught me about intuition and our connection to God, the Universe, Source, or The Great Spirit. (We each have our own word that feels 'right' to us.)

My mother told me that we all have angelic helpers and spirit guides, and she regularly sought support from hers. She encouraged me to reach out to mine and develop a connection of my own. Her lessons on gratitude and the importance of counting our blessings were told through this spiritual lens.

Consequently, I learned from a young age to view life's many challenges as opportunities to learn and grow, which has always served me well—especially through this transit of grief.

In these pages, you will recognize how I used this invaluable wisdom passed down from my mom, lighting the way through my darkest hours.

You will hear me talk about my Higher Self, True Self, and Divine Self. To me, these are interchangeable terms pointing to the divine essence within each of us. I also mention my small self or personality self, which refers to the human or earthly self. For me, true healing comes when we are able to honor and synthesize each of those aspects, bringing them into a harmonious whole.

In the pages that follow, we will begin in the darkest period of my journey through grief—the day of Claude's suicide, when there was no light at all in my sky. I will take you through my own highs and lows, and the many experiences that molded me into this *widow* I am today.

As the book progresses, my story of healing is interwoven with lessons, tools, automatic writing from my Higher Self and the angelic realm, communications with Claude, and signs and symbols from the natural world. All these aspects serve to support this multifaceted pilgrimage.

To begin, here's another inspirational message from my angelic guides:

*We are here to say that your life is not over. Actually, if you allow it, it is just the beginning of a new chapter. The old one, although it served you well at the time, is not in your highest interest anymore.*

Ultimately, this is a book about healing, hope, the resilience of our inner spirits, divine inspiration, and choice. As humans, we as a species have been given free will; therefore, the path we choose is always up to us. *We* get to decide how we will move through our loss. We can move through it with resistance or with grace—often experiencing some combination of the two, or something in between.

In my case, I first adapted by seizing the more masculine aspects of myself. As a single mom, I focused on the nuts and bolts of life, such as selling Claude's business, buying and selling properties and cars, and moving to another state.

As I gradually sought the support of healers and therapists, my divine feminine began to bloom, opening ever more to my intuitive divine nature. Eventually, I would even open my heart again to love.

I know how isolating grief can be, but I want you to know that you are not alone. My words are meant to compliment your unique inner work, done either on your own or with others assisting you. If at all possible, I highly endorse seeking support from professionals who are trained and equipped to work with grief, and, if needed, with trauma. This has been a critical choice for me. Without support, I imagine it would have felt like sinking in quicksand, without someone there to scoop me up. For me, flying solo wasn't an option. A loss by suicide is an additional brand of grief which adds another layer of tender heart-work to those who are faced with that extraordinary circumstance.

Between each chapter, I invite you to pause and take a breath with affirmations I have chosen. These can be used in those moments when you need a boost, helping you to shift into a more elevated perspective when that feels appropriate. In the back pages of this book, you will find a list of paid and free resources that have proven to be invaluable for me. My *Widow's Lunar Toolkit* can be accessed to further support your grieving process.

From the wisdom I've gained through these cycles of grief, I want you to know that we *all* have the capacity to unveil scores of shimmering stars from within, activating and illuminating our soul's path. My hope is that *Widow's Moon* will be one of those luminous stars, guiding your multifaceted passage to wholeness and healing.

# I

# SORROW

Claude started his day wearing a freshly-pressed, striped linen shirt and a pair of jeans. I remember thinking with a heavy heart that I had given him that shirt as a gift during a happier time, and that it was one of my favorites. As he approached the door to head to work, he paused, then slowly turned around to look at me. He seemed hesitant, but in a heartbeat, he was gone. Little did I know that precious moment would be the last time I saw him alive.

I will never forget the expression on his disheartened face.

Claude looked like a dog with his tail between his legs, utterly and totally beaten down. It was agonizing to see him that way. Yet I have to admit that even though I worried about him every minute of the day during that time, I felt a sense of relief when the door closed behind him. I could breathe again.

For nine months, I had watched my husband's gradual physical and emotional decline. I was caught up in his twisted perceptions of reality. The amount of energy it took to keep myself from falling down the rabbit hole with him was immense, and I had reached my limit.

The last two months of Claude's life were two of the most distressing months of mine, too. Claude was reviewing his past obsessively. Despite the fact that his company was thriving, he felt that he had failed as a businessman. He believed he'd lost his ability to lead and that a precipitous fall was ahead. His health was in decline, and he didn't think there was a way to improve it. Nothing I said or did reassured him. For that matter, nothing anyone did or said could impede his descent. It was hard to believe that things had become so critical that he had already spent three nights in a treatment center on suicide watch.

Once back home from that stay, the magnitude of the darkness that held him in its grasp reached a whole new level. For the following two weeks, Claude was not rational, and it was frightening to watch. The Claude I knew had been hijacked, as if he were possessed by some other dark force. He knew he had no power over it. One day he said to me with tears in his eyes, "I can't stop this. Believe me, I've tried."

His pessimistic conclusions about the 'unfixable' issues with his business sent him to even deeper levels of torment and shame. After almost fifteen years of the sustained and relentless pressures of business ownership, Claude had grown weary of the day-to-day office supervision and administration concerns. To remedy this, he chose to delegate more of the company's management to other employees so he could step back and carry less of the burden.

During the last few months of his life, he came to believe he had given up far too much unsupervised control to his employees. This resulted in some organizational issues, but due to his severely distorted perceptions, he viewed them as catastrophic to the health of the business when in reality they were things that just needed some alterations.

In a normal time, Claude would have simply stepped in to make the necessary changes. But to his mistaken mind, this would only add to the level of shame. In other words, he felt he was a captain who had lost his way. His ship was sinking uncontrollably, ever closer to its untimely demise. This perception in turn fed his fears around losing command of the narrative of his life and legacy, which he had worked so vigorously to achieve.

This false belief appeared to be the final insult to his sense of worth on the day he took his life.

Claude called me several times throughout that morning to express his distress and sorrow. He was a man teetering on the edge of oblivion. My attempts to soothe him were ineffective against the absolute authority of his fatalistic worldview. He seemed trapped in a nightmare with no hope of awakening.

Late in the afternoon, I was out grocery shopping while I waited for our son to finish his afterschool activity. I decided to give Claude a call to check in on him since he'd had such a harrowing day. He finally picked up after what felt like more than the maximum number of rings, sounding drained and depressed. I had grown accustomed to this over those many months of his waning health, but something felt a bit different this time. I couldn't quite put my finger on it. We had a brief conversation, and his last words were "I'll see you when you get home." I was hesitant to finish the call, but I cautiously decided to trust that he would be ok.

Noah and I arrived there about an hour later. We pulled into the garage beside Claude's car. I noticed right away that he didn't come out to greet us as he normally would. This felt particularly unsettling, since we had an understanding in our house that Claude actually established in our early years together. On a typical day, the agreement was that when one of us arrived home, the other would drop what we were doing. We would then greet each other with hugs and kisses. It was a sweet and loving ritual that we strictly followed. Though his absence felt concerning, based on our phone conversation, I told myself that he must be sleeping.

Though logically valid, that story didn't hold up for long. The lack of greeting wasn't the only thing that felt off. As I walked into the kitchen with groceries in hand, I noticed the energy in the house—it seemed hauntingly still and quiet. Despite sensing this, I made the decision to stay on track and put the groceries away before I looked in on Claude. I was feeling fairly stressed, so I opened a nice cool beer and poured it into a glass to help take the edge off. I took a few refreshing gulps, and I could immediately feel the effects of the alcohol helping to calm my nerves. When I was finished putting everything away, I paused and took a deep breath.

I needed to take a moment to prepare myself to be with Claude. I walked to our bedroom, assuming I would find him resting there. When I opened the door, my heart sunk. I saw that the bed was untouched, still perfectly made up from that morning. There was no sign of Claude and no evidence that he had even been in there at all. It seemed likely in that moment that the unthinkable may have happened. He must have done it—he must have killed himself. On the one hand, I thought he would never actually commit this act, yet it was also my worst fear, considering his state of mind.

I could feel my whole body going into fight-or-flight mode. My heart was racing. I called to Noah, who was about to go into the shower, "Where is your dad?"

He replied "I don't know" with a typical teenage tone that implied he felt it was a silly question to ask. I was trying not to panic, but my mind was starting to paint the picture of the worst-case scenario. What else was I to think?

I frantically searched each room of our 3,000 square-foot house. I started with the downstairs bedrooms. We typically kept the doors closed, so it was like a video game or a frightening dream. I wondered, *Which door will lead to his dead body? How did he do it? Will it be bloody?* With every step and every forceful beat of my heart, my apprehension grew as I opened each door, not knowing what I would find.

When I didn't find him on the first floor, my mind briefly said, *Maybe he's at a neighbor's house.* It was trying to calm itself down by creating another unrealistic story. Claude had not been to any neighbor's house in months. He was too much of an emotional mess for that. Then I thought, *I must be overreacting. Everything will be fine. He would never hurt himself. He's terrified of dying.* I was desperate to create a narrative that made sense.

But it was finally sinking in that I wasn't imagining the unfading quiet in the house that I'd felt earlier. It was as if that stillness had a life of its own; it seemed deafening.

I headed up the stairs to check the last two bedrooms. The first one was Noah's room. I thought, *Surely he wouldn't do it in there.* I opened the door and briefly felt a sense of relief. But then I realized that I had one more room to check, and it was directly behind me. Looking back on this memory, it was like a horror film. This was literally the turning point—the moment when you are watching the main character, afraid to look at what she is about to discover.

I noticed right away the door to my art studio was left half open. My heart sunk even deeper; I always left that door closed.

Filled with apprehension, I walked across the long bridge that overlooked the living room on one side and the front entranceway on the other. The late afternoon sun was streaming in through the skylights. As I stepped into my studio, I instantly felt the door bump into the attic door that was sandwiched up against it on the other side. Entering the room, I found the attic door was wide open. Behind it, Claude's lifeless body was hanging by a rope from the rafter.

In the finality of that moment, I felt exceedingly horrified and angry. I thought *How could you do this, Claude? You're dead now! You can't take this back!*

Talk about a scene from a horror film. I stood there trembling with absolute disbelief as my husband hung in the darkened attic, completely motionless. The hangdog look from that morning was imprinted onto his pale wax-like face. He looked utterly defeated.

My beloved husband was gone. All that I was left with in that inconceivable instant was his body and the memory of who he once was. My heart had shattered entirely, and I found myself screaming loudly, more loudly than I had ever thought possible, *No!* Then I heard an inner voice say with urgency, *Stop screaming right now and call the police. You can't let Noah see this.*

I had only been with Claude for maybe thirty seconds when I heard that penetrating voice. I turned as if I were under a spell, an unseen force. I managed to shamble back across the bridge, knowing I had to make my way downstairs.

I was in shock, crying and shaking. I found myself repeating "Oh my God." I thought *He's really done this, he's gone.* At the same time, I was filled with disbelief. How could this be real? *This is what happens to other people or on TV.*

By the time I had gotten to the bottom of the stairs, a wave of relief washed over me, soon followed by one of guilt. My worst fear had been realized, yet the weight I had been carrying for months was released. The nightmare was over. The pain was excruciating, yet I felt numb.

I knew I had to keep it together, just keep moving one foot in front of the other to make that 911 call. I was following a directive. The woman on the other end of the phone picked up right away. I was crying and I said the unthinkable words, "My husband hung himself." She was insistent that I stay on the line until an officer arrived. The first one seemed to arrive instantaneously. Within fifteen minutes, there were so many people in my house that I didn't know who was who.

Not long after, Noah emerged from his shower dressed in his pajamas. He was completely oblivious and had no idea that his father had taken his life. Everything had happened so fast while he was divinely protected in the sanctity of his shower. Despite this, he told me years later that he did hear something as I was screaming. But he mistakenly thought it may have been the sound of a dog, so he paid it no mind. This leads me to believe that it was not part of his soul's path to experience the trauma of seeing his father's body.

In that split second, I had to tell my fourteen-year-old son that the father he adored was gone. There was no time to figure out how to say it. I just blurted out the words "your dad hung himself." Noah's eyes opened wide, and that was his only reaction. I didn't have time to really process this understated response.

The police officers asked us to leave while they conducted their investigation. I had the stark realization that our home was now officially considered a crime scene. My next-door neighbor whisked us away to her house while the police proceeded with the task at hand. Soon, I had three police officers plus a clergyman hovering around me. Two were the detectives assigned to the case, and they questioned me individually about what had happened. A woman police officer attentively held my hand as I sat there shaking. I was grateful and felt unexpectedly cared for while we waited for them to finish up at our house.

Most of what happened during that time is a blur to me, but I do remember clutching the portable home phone I still held in my hands from that 911 call. I felt startled as the phone suddenly rang. It was one of my closest friends, Aztechan, who lived out of state. We hadn't talked in a few months, so this felt bizarrely synchronistic. I was horrified to have to tell her what Claude had done yet comforted by the sound of her voice. We had all lived together for a time in California several years prior. She was at Noah's birth and is his godmother. I wondered later if Claude had arranged that call from the other side—his way of sending support at a time when he couldn't be there for me.

After nearly five hours, the investigation was over, and we were told by one of the detectives standing alongside the clergyman that they had declared his death a suicide. Even though that seemed obvious, it was still a relief to hear them say that. We were allowed to go back into our home, which of course would never feel the same again.

With a feeling of intense resistance, I was then faced with the task of letting my mother-in-law know that her son had just died by suicide. Maybe I should have called her right away, but I just couldn't bring myself to do it amidst the flurry of chaotic activity. I knew she was very private, so I guess I had been trying to protect her from the frenzy of those past five hours. I thought it best to tell her in person.

Noah and I walked over to her place, which was right around the corner from our house. It felt good to move, but I started crying and shaking again. I thought, *How can I tell Claude's mom what he did?* I knew it would shatter her heart just as it did mine. Noah was surprisingly calm and reassuring just like Claude would have been. At only fourteen years old, he was my momentary rock to cling to as we made our way to her condo.

After delivering the unimaginable news, I sat with her as she cried. I happened to notice our wedding photo on the bookshelf across from where we were sitting. I heard Claude's voice clearly say, "I regretted doing this as soon as my spirit left my body. I'm so sorry."

This didn't surprise me at all. I knew how much he loved and adored us. In his right mind, he never would have wanted to leave us. I think that when he passed, he woke up from his dark night. He was free and could see things clearly for the first time in months.

But this was it for him; his life as he knew it with us was over. We were now left to deal with the repercussions of that unalterable act.

On April 19, 2012, I officially entered this dark phase of the Widow's Moon. In the blink of an eye, I became a single mom and a survivor of suicide. I had absolutely no idea what I would do next and what my life would look like. Without any advance notice, I found myself living in uncharted territory with no GPS and no roadmap. I would have to find my way through this without Claude by my side for the first time in eighteen years.

*I honor and love the widow within.*
*I grieve, I cry,*
*I scream, I wail, I let it All out!*

# 2

# PRELUDE

T he beginning of our love story was more like a rom-com than a horror movie. How had it come to this?

It wasn't quite love at first sight when we met in San Francisco in 1994. Claude had recently moved to the city from Half Moon Bay where he had been injured in a car accident. He was referred to the chiropractic clinic where I was working as a massage therapist.

After fifteen years of doing bodywork, I established my own individual style of healing, incorporating intuitive energy work with massage. With this approach, I was accustomed to helping people go into a deep, trance-like state. I had studied massage and many other healing modalities while living in Santa Fe, New Mexico for five years in the mid-to-late '80s, where I also got my Reiki 1-2 certifications. When I moved to San Francisco in 1989, I furthered my studies in Mill Valley at The Academy of Intuitive Studies, now called The Academy of Intuition Medicine. There, I learned even more about working with our energetic bodies.

With Claude, all that training went out the window. For one thing, he chitchatted throughout our sessions. At first, I thought he was flirting with me. Because of this, I found him to be a bit annoying and irreverent.

During one of his weekly therapeutic massages, he commented on the music I typically played. In particular, he liked the sound of the water intermixed with the soothing melodies. This sparked the idea of inviting me on a relaxing weekend outing with some of his friends to sail the waters of San Francisco Bay. He said he thought I would unquestionably enjoy a relaxing day on the boat.

He was my massage client, and I really wasn't sure if I even liked him, so I was hesitant to say yes. I didn't know what his intentions were, either. Was he asking me out on a date? The idea made me uncomfortable, and the whole situation felt awkward. In fact, I was so taken by surprise I didn't even give him an answer! I was like a deer caught in headlights.

Soon, the massage was over, and I still hadn't responded. Why couldn't I give him the common courtesy of letting him know one way or the other? It was embarrassing.

Despite my blunder, there was something about his invitation that preoccupied my thoughts as the day progressed. I just couldn't let it go. After sitting with it for several hours, I felt compelled to accept. I mustered up all my courage to pick up the phone and dial his number knowing full well that he may reject me. After stalling for a few minutes and seeming clearly annoyed with me, he began counting out loud how many people had accepted his invitation to see if he had any more room. Though he sounded hesitant—and who could blame him—he then told me that I was still welcome to join them.

At this point, I was still clueless as to why making that call felt so important. But soon enough, it would all become clear.

It turned out to be an amazing day. The weather was spectacular, and I got to see another side of Claude. I witnessed a true transformation in his demeanor within his sailing domain. He seemed to fully embody his power and joy while on the water. I observed over time that being on the boat was his gateway to Spirit, aligning him to his true essence.

That day, I saw Claude's capacity for patience and generosity for those of us who were new to sailing. He was a great conversationalist, and his quick wit was on par with that of Jon Stewart.

I have to say, seeing him this way was a turn-on, and I knew that I was interested in him as a potential partner. I was thirty-seven, and it had been seven years since my first marriage ended in divorce. I'd had two relationships and briefly dated some others during that period, but nobody felt quite right as a life partner. My clock was ticking, and I was ready for love!

After a full day of sailing, Claude asked if anyone wanted to go out for some Thai food. I secretly hoped that they would decline so I could have him all to myself. I got my wish, and it felt meant to be. We really hit it off; the conversation flowed easily, and I discovered more facets of Claude's personality. His intelligence, depth, sensitivity, and compassion were becoming clearer to me as we continued talking. He shared some details about his troubled childhood growing up in the projects in Manhattan, and I learned that he had spent many years in therapy working through his issues that were a result of his traumatic childhood experiences. Having spent many years in therapy myself and being a proponent of personal growth, I had a lot of respect for his dedication to healing wounds from the past. This was an important factor in choosing a partner for myself.

I was astonished and truly blown away.

After dinner, Claude invited me up to his apartment for a cup of tea to continue our discussion. It felt like we could have talked all night. However, it was getting late, so we said goodbye quite innocently with a warm embrace. As I drove home to the other side of San Francisco, my whole body was filled with excitement and anticipation. I got little sleep after that magical day and night. As I tossed and turned, I kept thinking that this could be it; he could be "the one I have been waiting for!"

I repeatedly held myself back from calling him the next day. Instead, I decided to write him a thank you note. He called me right away after reading it. He told me that he was impressed that I took the initiative to not only thank him but to also invite him out again— so much so that we made a plan to get together for the upcoming weekend for brunch.

While I anxiously awaited his arrival for our first official date at Half Day Café, I received two images intuitively. I saw that he would bring me flowers, and I saw what our first kiss would look like. From an early age, I recognized that I have four 'clair' senses. I am clairvoyant, which is intuitive clear seeing or inner sight. This ability allows me to see mental images in my mind's eye, third eye, or my 'intuitive center.' I am clairaudient, which means that I have the ability to hear sounds or words broadcast from the etheric realm. Added to the mix is clairsentience, which is the intuitive ability to sense and clearly feel subtle energy around me. Finally, I am claircognizant. My intuitive, clear knowing gives me the ability to gain spiritual insights or knowledge from Spirit or to receive premonitions of something that may happen in the future. In summary, I am a highly sensitive, intuitive empath.

These abilities have assisted me in innumerable ways on my healing journey, and they were accurate on that occasion, too. When I opened the door, I saw that Claude was standing there holding in his arms not one, but two dozen purple roses. I was ecstatic, as this was considerably above and beyond what I had imagined. Clearly, he was feeling as much anticipation as I was about the potential that our connection held. It also was beyond a doubt a confirmation of the first image I had received.

After brunch, neither of us was ready for the date to end, so we decided to drive up to nearby Mount Tamalpais (or as the locals call it, Mount Tam) for a short hike. I started to notice a queasy sensation in my belly which was only enhanced by that road with its twists and turns leading up to the trailhead. I wasn't sure if I should take the risk of sharing my feelings, but I thought *let's see how he responds to this*.

I said to him "I'm really scared." He asked me why and I said, "I *really* like you."

To my surprise and joy he said the exact same thing right back to me.

We reached the parking lot, got out of the car, and found a spot to sit by the side of the trail. He held me and said, "I have to warn you about something." He went on, "you know … if we're going to do this, we're going to do it all. Marriage … the white picket fence … the kids, et cetera."

I was speechless. Was I hearing him correctly? Had I now entered the Twilight Zone? This was exactly what I wanted, but I didn't expect him to declare it so quickly. Despite this, I said, "Yes, I'm in, let's do it" without hesitation. It may sound crazy, but it just felt right.

After that declaration of our future intentions, we took a short walk holding hands along the trail. He stopped suddenly, and with a swoop and a dip, he held me for our first kiss. It was purely romantic and just the way I had seen it in my mind's eye.

Claude's foretelling of our future that singular day on Mount Tam soon became our reality. From the start, we were on the fast track to creating our lives together. Beginning with falling in love posthaste, we were married a year later on the Pacific coastline.

That day was infused with anticipation and stunning clear blue skies on the Northern California coast. Enhanced by the sound of the crashing ocean waves below us, we said our wedding vows surrounded by an intimate group of family and friends. It was picture perfect. Was our life together picture perfect? I would have to use one of Claude's favorite phrases, "not so much." Yet, would I do it all over again knowing the future outcome? Yes, I would. We rode the waves of our relationship with immutable love and a consummate commitment to our marriage. We laughed (a lot), we cried (also a lot), and we co-created a life that we could be proud of.

We went onto home buying, parenthood, and even moved to a new state to start a business, all within a five-year period. We both possessed the capacity to carry a vision to its completion, which made us a good team. Taking risks and trusting even through various degrees of fear and uncertainty is a learned behavior and a practice. Prior to meeting, we both had our share of opportunities with this in our lives, so we understood one another on that level.

We began our marriage living in a two-bedroom townhome in the coastal community of Pacifica, California. Claude was a sales rep and managed the satellite office in San Francisco for a company that has offices worldwide in the trade show industry. Only seventeen miles south of San Francisco, the location was ideal for commuting and for easy entry to the city. In addition to that, as a nature lover, I especially valued the convenient accessibility to the beaches and hiking trails. Driving down the coast to spend time in Moss Beach, Half Moon Bay, Monterey, and Big Sur were some of our favorite excursions on the weekends. Sailing on San Francisco Bay, or as he used to call it, "scooting around the bay," remained central to our recreational activities. It was a joyous time, and we frequently acknowledged how grateful we were to have one another and to live in that highly desirable slice of heaven.

As I settled into married life and established my own massage therapy practice, the urge to start a family soon blossomed. I became pregnant fairly quickly, but in the first trimester we lost our little one. We knew we wanted to try again, but we decided to wait a few months to regain a positive outlook after our painful loss. Soon enough, we were blessed with another pregnancy; however, there were some medical issues which made this one a high risk for me and the baby. I was more than willing to make any necessary sacrifices to keep our baby healthy. Sadly, that meant I had to stop working in my massage practice and limit the time on my feet to no more than twenty minutes.

Noah, our "beautiful miracle baby" as the doctors called him, was born in 1998 healthy and strong via caesarean birth. He was, to use another one of Claude's familiar phrases, "without question" the love of our lives.

After about a year, it became clear that we were outgrowing our living space and wanted to transition from our townhome to a house with a yard to raise our son. Much to our dismay, the real estate prices in California had become exceedingly high. We had just begun exploring other options when *seemingly* out of the blue, Claude was presented with a new business venture. The law of attraction was surely at play here.

Claude was being offered the chance to buy one of the state dealerships in Memphis, Tennessee with a satellite office in Little Rock, Arkansas. Though Tennessee was not a place that would have ever been on our radar, it really did feel like the Universe dropped this into our laps. It was too good an opportunity to pass up.

Living in the Mid-South would be a major cultural difference for us. Being inland, there were no large bodies of water, which meant no sailing for Claude. I truly loved and had grown accustomed to living on the coast and in close proximity to the mountains for the previous ten years. There would be no access to either of those in our new home other than by extended car trips or air flight. We both knew how important these outlets were for us, but we moved forward despite our reservations. Claude's professional dreams and ambitions overshadowed any thoughts of potential challenges that we might encounter with this new direction. We jointly decided that we would try it out for at least five years. If we hated it, we would move again and start another chapter. Little did we know at the time how hard it would be to follow through on that promise.

The five-year mark came and went. Though we were supremely fortunate to have a prosperous business, neither of us was particularly happy in our overall life circumstances. But all things considered, we felt we needed to stay the course; it was the practical financial choice after all. We were living what many think of as the American Dream: a husband with a successful career and a red brick house in the suburbs at the end of a cul-de-sac, surrounded by trees with a pool in the back yard. Eventually, we would acquire two little white poodles that Noah begged us for when he was six years old to complete the picture-perfect life.

But I have to say that, true to our prediction, living that life was not really *our* dream. Claude felt like a fish out of water, and I felt like a stranger in a strange land.

Not long after our move, I made the decision to be a stay-at-home mom. My body was tired after being a massage therapist for all those fifteen years, and I was an older parent, almost forty-one when Noah was born. Though I had imagined that I would never give up my healing practice since it was a passion of mine to help others, I wanted to put my full attention into raising our eighteen-month-old son. In addition to my primary focus on mommy duty, I had begun the process of making our house our *home*.

As Noah grew older, homeschooling became the best course of action for grades 2-7. Right around pre-school we became aware of his disruptive behavior issues. By kindergarten, we had him evaluated and learned he had ADHD, Sensory Integration Disorder, some auditory processing issues, and an IQ that was in the highly-gifted range. Though he was not officially diagnosed with Asperger's during that time, he had demonstrated some tendencies on that spectrum socially which he has spent much of his teen and adult life refining.

Never in my wildest dreams would I have ever imagined becoming a homeschool mom. It was a monumental responsibility and undertaking, but through a lot of trial and error, we figured it all out and made it work to best of our ability. Ultimately, this was the best choice in the big picture of Noah's life. It also helped me develop a closer bond with him, which would prove invaluable after Claude's suicide.

Time passed, and Claude and I both found home remodeling to be a satisfying creative outlet. At thirteen, Noah started feeling that he was ready to give school another try for the eighth grade. After three attempts over the years to get him into one highly desirable private school, he made it in. The third time was the charm. There, he was able to easily develop close friendships and the teachers seemed to appreciate his unique qualities. These were all huge milestones for him at the time.

2011 was an impactful and transitional year for all of us. For Noah and I, it was one of new and exciting beginnings. Being released from my homeschooling duties freed me up to start putting more of my efforts into my artwork and showing my paintings. I was an art major in college, but after graduation, I never allowed myself to fully engage with it in any meaningful way or for any length of time. During the two years prior to Claude's suicide I had created a body of work and was on a trajectory of starting to get my artwork into the world. I had my first solo show five months before his death with others to follow. I felt excited and committed to that path. For Noah, starting back at school after six years was an enormous breakthrough. But for Claude, it was an entirely different story. For him, 2011 was the beginning of a decline that led to his final transition from this life.

*I am brave,*
*I can do this,*
*one step,*
*one moment,*
*one breath at time.*

# 3

# DESCENT

Noah and I were urged by our neighbors and friends not to sleep at our house that first night after Claude's suicide. I hadn't had the presence of mind to look that far ahead while caught in the emotional whirlwind of the previous several hours, but they were right, of course. It would have been way too much, way too soon. Even though I wanted nothing more than to seek refuge in the comfort of my own bed, Claude's passing had changed everything. Nothing about being in my home that night would have felt comforting.

Before I knew it, that plan of action was fully mobilized, orchestrated by our neighbors and friends. We needed to collect some of our belongings, which meant we had to go back into the house. It felt disorienting walking through the front door, the gateway to my new reality. The stark realization hit me that just hours before, Claude's body had been wheeled out on a gurney right where I was standing. It felt surreal and unsettling. I went straight ahead into the living room and paused. I found myself looking up to the doorway of my art studio knowing the attic was just beyond that. It felt dreamlike, and I wondered how this could have happened to our sweet family.

The friends who came to help us seemed incredibly brave in my eyes. I thought surely it must have felt uncomfortable for them, but not a word was spoken about it. They stayed focused on the task at hand and followed me around my house like a litter of puppies, all of them chattering like nothing had happened. I even joined in a few times myself, cracking a few jokes.

I thought to myself; *this would have been Claude's manner of coping.* His quick wit was second nature to him. Could inserting humor have been something he felt he could do for me from the other side to help ease my pain? I found it all rather bizarre. Despite that, I played along. I knew it was a momentary deviation from the reality we were facing and was probably a good thing to help us all get through this difficult situation.

Once Noah and I were ready to go, we were whisked away in two separate cars to what felt like our own individual safe houses insulated from the outside world. Noah went to his friend Ariana's house to find his respite there. I landed just a few doors down with Grace, one of Claude's long-time employees and friends. At that point, it was around midnight. I settled into an unfamiliar room that I felt no connection to. It felt odd but safe, and I was grateful to have this time alone after the most intense night of my life. It gave me the space I needed to take a breath, figure out my next move, and allow the integration process to begin.

I think I may have just sat there in shock on the bed for at least two hours before attempting to sleep. This was one of the few times that I would have welcomed having some pharmaceutical assistance. Haunting flashbacks persisted through the entire night. Every time I closed my eyes, all I could see was Claude's face while he hung in that dingy, dark attic.

Claude and I had an undeniable connection and loved each other deeply. Nonetheless, our relationship was complex, fraught with highs and lows and everything in between. It was clear that our partnership would serve an important purpose for us both at a soul level—in life and through death. It was a seemingly perfect match for shining a light on our shadow parts, leading to growth and transformation. The emotional triggers brought to the surface in our marriage were at times overwhelming, and more than we could carry on our own. Because of this, we repeatedly sought support through couple's counseling over the years. We eventually learned that our issues were really all about what was unresolved within ourselves rather being either person's "fault." Through all those ups and downs, our love deepened, and our relationship grew and evolved.

Once we moved to Tennessee, Claude's business took the majority of his attention and focus, especially during those early years. Despite that, he was considerate enough in his dedication as a husband and father to always prioritize spending time with us. Due to the indelible memories from his difficult childhood with an alcoholic, absentee father, he was determined to show up as best as he could for us both.

Yet how could I not help but feel that I was in some part responsible for his decline? In the days following his death, I ran through the events of the prior year in my head again and again.

Claude freely gave of himself and his affection. Aside from my mom, Claude was my biggest cheerleader. He had an endless supply of encouragement for me and saw my strengths beyond what I could recognize in myself back then. At times, it would result in considerable frustration on his part, but he persisted, helping me through my difficult, stubborn moments when I lacked confidence of my own. He would say on many occasions that "you are a strong and powerful woman and you can do anything you put your mind to." After he died, I found an old Mother's Day card he had given me that read "If you are capable of Noah you are capable of anything."

Though his unwavering belief in me was a gift, it sometimes felt like a double-edged sword. He could see things in me that had not been developed yet. To put it simply, he saw my potential. However, at times it felt uncomfortable; there was pressure to be someone that

I was not ready to be *yet*. And now, after his death, I had no choice but to be ready.

I knew Claude to be a highly resilient and resourceful man. I used to call him a master of manifestation. He was highly intuitive and followed his own inner guidance system while running his business in a rather unconventional way. He pushed the boundaries with his tenacity and seemingly limitless resolve. He innately knew how to adapt and to be in the flow, rolling with the punches. If he didn't know how to do something, he found someone who could help him do it.

He had already faced trial by fire innumerable times with his business, figuratively and literally. Claude housed his business in a building that he owned, located in a historic district of downtown Memphis. One bitterly cold winter night, a homeless man started a fire to stay warm on the premises. Sadly, it spread and burned out of control. The end result was a complete loss of not only the structure, but also everything in it, including all of the valuable trade show merchandise that was stored there.

After the initial shock, Claude promptly began the arduous process of reconstructing his business foundations, from the bottom up. Claude was a true warrior who came out ahead and stronger for the experience. He was told by his colleagues that many would not have had the strength and determination that he had shown during that time. He faced many things in his life this way.

Yet despite the inner strength that lifted him up innumerable times, the man I married was slowly and progressively disappearing for many years preceding his death. The pressures of managing and owning a business took their toll on his emotional and physical health. In addition to that, he was conflicted about the way he was spending the most valuable currency, his life. On one hand, he was grateful for all that he had: a thriving business that he could be proud of, a wife that he was still in love with, a son that he adored more than life itself.

On the other, something important was missing. It is a story that we hear so often in our human experience.

Claude was not a spiritual or religious man, so he did not derive any solace in having a higher awareness to help him put things into perspective. Time slipped away as we spent thirteen years living in a city we both felt dissatisfied with. We were there solely for the business opportunity. It met our financial needs, but not our personal needs. Consequently, we began to feel trapped. This might sound strange, but as I write this, I am seeing that he was progressively drying up over those years we lived inland—slowly losing his life force and in turn his will to live. We would visit the coast from time to time to remedy that, but clearly it wasn't enough. I realize now that he needed that direct connection as if his very existence depended on it. As I'd observed that first time on his sailboat, the ocean was a lifeline to his soul.

While caught in the cycles of grief, I have discovered that we need our *lifelines* more than ever. Without them, we can feel lightyears away from others. Our world can feel meaningless and totally eclipsed by our pain.

Our *lifelines* won't take the pain away, but they can help us stay afloat minute by minute, day by day. They may even inspire us and illuminate our steps as we move forward, embracing our new reality.

We talked on numerous occasions about redesigning our lives. We discussed selling the business and moving to a new location where Claude could have a sailboat and I could have greater access to natural beauty. We wanted to recapture the magic of what we had when we first met. But nothing ever changed. Ultimately, Claude's life was out of balance on multiple levels. He was off course and seemed almost impotent to make the changes we yearned for. Though he explored various options, he couldn't create a viable plan to make the transition to a new business opportunity that he felt comfortable with. I continually felt perplexed by this.

How could my husband, who was a master at finding solutions to just about anything, not find his way out of this situation?

In his attempts to make peace with our decision to stay, he passed through a series of phases. During each cycle, he would access renewed levels of creativity, inspiration, and resolve to keep moving forward, improving his business each time. He did his best to create a new relationship to something that no longer felt fulfilling as it once had. I supported him implicitly, but I saw the degree of anguish he went through, so I always concluded my words of support with "as long as you will feel at peace with your decision and you won't let it kill you." That might sound extreme, but it was a disturbing, recurring thought at the time.

The financial crisis of 2008, as it turned out, was the best thing that could have happened to us from a financial perspective. The trade show industry was booming. The previous version of Claude, the one who was still passionate about running his business, would have been on cloud nine. The business was on its most profitable trajectory since he had taken ownership a full nine years earlier. We were enormously fortunate but felt more entrenched than ever. How could we leave a flourishing business in that economic climate?

Yet the stresses of the business growing so rapidly when he would have rather been spending his life force energy in other ways were a drag on his system on all levels. His health was progressively weakening.

Claude had a history of Crohn's, an inflammatory bowel disease. This seemed to worsen over those years due to multiple stress factors. He had mood, cholesterol, and even sleep issues. He was taking prescription medications for all of these maladies. Some occasional back pain threw another drug into the mix. It seems clear to me looking back that he was not living his life in alignment with his soul purpose.

Nine months before Claude's suicide, he went in for his routine colonoscopy. His doctor was exceptionally pleased with the test results and he added that he wouldn't have suspected that Claude had Crohn's disease at all. In light of that assertion, we were dismayed two weeks later when he started to feel pain in his lower abdomen. His doctor thought it must have been a flare up of his Crohn's and put Claude on six weeks of steroids. More pharmaceuticals!

Shortly thereafter, living with him was like living in an alternate universe. Claude was normally easygoing, gentle, loving, and supportive. However, due to the side effects of the steroids, I found him to be arrogant, critical, controlling, and manic. Where did my husband go?

Claude scrutinized everything I said or did. It felt like I was living in a minefield. It was a trying time, yet little did I know that the worst was on the horizon.

He was never quite the same after that round of meds. The steroids were not alleviating his abdominal pain, so his doctor decided to prescribe him another anti-inflammatory medication. This one arrived at our doorstep in a cooler with an injection pen inside. I opened up the box and read the ominous list of the possible side effects—lymphoma and death were among the worst. I was horrified. To this day, when I see this medication advertised on TV, I feel nauseated.

I expressed my worries to Claude as gently as possible. I said, "this is really hard for me, watching you take all these potentially harmful medications."

He responded with anger; "I need you to be supportive of me right now. This is what the doctor prescribed, so I'm going to take it." I could hear the desperation in his voice after months of trying multiple things to mitigate his pain without any actual results.

I was in a very delicate position. I wanted more than anything to support Claude's healing. However, my methods of choice were the exact opposite of Claude's. I would have preferred a more natural and holistic approach, but that wasn't Claude's way. Regrettably, I felt I needed to honor and respect his wishes. He was more comfortable putting his faith in and following the advice of the more traditional medical model.

After twelve weeks following those recommendations and taking two types of anti-inflammatory and immunosuppressant medications with no relief, his doctor concluded that he must have Irritable Bowel Syndrome or IBS. Subsequently, he treated Claude with anti-anxiety and anti-depressant drugs. Nothing was helping; he was still in pain. Over those months, Claude developed significant sleep dysfunction and lost twenty pounds. He became despondent and hopeless. Who wouldn't?

This was a hellish existence for us both. I withstood nine months of standing by helplessly while Claude turned to various medical professionals for help with no results. In that time, he slowly lost his mental and physical health, and ultimately his will to live. He was on a slippery slope, and I felt helpless against the forces that held him captive. Noah was losing his dad, and I was losing my husband. The anti-psychotic drugs that were given to him while on suicide watch seemed to be the final blow. Within a month, he would end his own life.

During the last few weeks of Claude's life, he was barely functioning due to sleep deprivation and his delusional state of mind. We spent hours just sitting together. He said to me one day: "I feel like I'm preparing to die." I wasn't sure how to take that. Was he overreacting due to his weakened mind and body, or was he on some level seeing what lay ahead?

Though this was the darkest cycle we had faced together, our love endured. In this shadow-ridden phase, I now see the gifts that we were able to access. This was the most tender and intimate moment in time we had ever shared as one. Claude was emotionally raw and unfiltered. Through it all, because of my steadfast and loving presence, he repeatedly said to me "you are a saint." Our hearts were completely open and filled with pure unconditional love for one another. Any unresolved conflicts or issues that still stood between simply melted away. For this reason, I will always cherish that period of time and view it as his final gift to me.

Still, I wished that I had been able to change the course of those events. Soon after, all our realities would change forever.

Lying in bed that first night after several unbearable sleepless hours, I found a way to consciously suppress some of the horror as Claude's face returned to me again and again. I thought, *why not try blocking out his face with that circular white film like you see on documentary movies when they want to hide someone's identity?* It was so effective that to this day, I can't remember exactly what his face looked like. I have had glimpses, but the clear picture has never fully returned. This is not to say that I've been sheltered from all the effects of the trauma from finding him. Far from it! This one piece, however, is locked away in my subconscious mind. It was more than my heart and psyche could handle, so I did what I could to shield myself from that part of the experience.

I managed to doze off for maybe two hours living through that hellish night. I woke up early the next morning with a massive migraine and an upset stomach, feeling like I had been hit by a Mack truck. I had the sense that my heart was pulling at my lungs, making it hard to breathe.

I awoke to a new day, a new physical reality. My dear Claude was gone. *How could this be true?* I thought. Dragging myself out of bed, I began shuffling around the house aimlessly at a snail's pace, dazed and confused.

Despite my current vantage point, there was a glimmer of the woman who Claude knew could rise above it all. The one who could take on the world with her inner strength. She would keep me moving at a time when there seemed to be no will or momentum as I carried the full weight and influence of the Widow's Moon.

*I am loving & gentle*
*with myself as*
*I find my way through grief.*

# 4

# RECLAMATION

E ven as I faced the magnitude of this loss, I recognized that I was extremely fortunate. About a year prior to his suicide, Claude had assembled a team of people who would be readily available should something happen to him. Since we had our estate planning fully in order, I was prepared and knew exactly who to call. They, in turn, set all of the balls in motion. I had assistance every step of the way through the web of banking, real estate, legal affairs, and the task of keeping the business up and running in his absence. In an ironic twist, the autonomy Claude gave his employees turned out to be a saving grace rather than a damning mistake.

That first day, I began this process with what seemed like an endless number of phone calls, all while feeling utterly sleep deprived and at the lowest point of my life.

By day three, I'd had two restless nights and was beyond ready to be back in my own space again. My hideaway had served me well. Now, I knew with every fiber of my being what my next steps needed to be. It wouldn't be easy to set foot in our house again, but I was highly motivated to start the process of reclaiming our home from the horror of what had happened.

I felt relieved and appreciative to know that my brother, Bill, and his wife, Leslie, would fly in that day from Massachusetts to lend their loving support. After picking them up from the airport, our first stop was Whole Foods. I wanted to make sure that we had everything we needed while they were in town. But I hadn't been out from my protective cocoon in two-and-a-half days, so I was feeling particularly vulnerable. I stood in the produce section in front of a huge mound of sweet potatoes feeling completely overwhelmed. I froze momentarily, standing there motionless. I thought *how can everyone just be going about their business?* My outrage was on the brink of erupting. In my mind's eye, I imagined my own version of one of the signature scenes from the Ally McBeal TV show. In this episodic fantasy, I saw myself with wildly flailing arms, sweeping all the produce onto the floor and climbing up on that produce table to yell, "What's wrong with all of you? Don't you know what happened!?" Seeing that scenario streaming in my mind was kind of alarming, yet mildly humorous. Of course, I had no intention of indulging my unrestrained vision. I kept quiet and continued with my inner struggle to stay focused on the task at hand.

Looking back, I see this as a perfect example of the grief-ridden stupor we may inevitably find ourselves residing in after we lose someone dear to us.

In a perfect world, it would have been preferable to avoid ever having to set foot back in that house given the way Claude died. However, there were many factors that played into my decision to stay. First, this was the home that Claude and I spent years lovingly creating. It was where our son grew up. I wasn't going to let one tragic day in our lives take away the importance of those things. After settling in, I soon learned that in some ways it actually felt comforting to remain because of all the happy memories that were made there. Second, I had the sense that a move to another state was in our near future, but I wasn't sure when. I couldn't wrap my mind around moving twice. Third, I knew it would take a lot of time, energy, and effort to get my house ready to put on the market. I was in no condition to do any of that. Just getting up each morning and getting through each day took tremendous effort and determination. I needed to focus all of my energy on taking care of Noah and our two dogs, plus settling all the business and estate dealings, *plus* taking care of my own needs. Moving at that point was absolutely out of the question.

I needed to make this work. I was determined to do whatever I could to make it feel like a safe haven once again.

I already knew that rooms and houses can hold energy from past and present circumstances. For my mental and physical health, it felt imperative for me to clear the toxic energy resulting from the previous months. Between Claude's illness and his suicide, I had my work cut out for me. My goal was to update and attune our home to a present time frequency which would be more supportive to my healing process. With Bill and Leslie's help, I began by clearing out Claude's walk-in closet in the master bath. I didn't want to sort through any of it; I found it too painful. I just wanted it gone.

Erasing all signs of Claude's existence was not my intention. Besides, that would have been impossible. His energy was sewn and stitched into the very fabric of our home. But the conscious decision to reclaim my living space as soon as possible was an essential component to my grieving and healing process. It helped me feel like I was in control of something in my life at a time when everything felt *out* of control.

We filled up the van with Claude's clothing and donated all of it. Although removing Claude's belongings was upsetting, I could already feel myself breathing a little easier with all of that soul-crushing energy out of the house.

Since I had knowledge of some basic energy clearing techniques, I used sage, essential oil sprays, and prayer as I invited my angels to enter our home and fill it with love, light, and blessings.

But eventually, I had to face the attic.

I knew from the start that if I was going to heal this trauma, I had to meet my fears head-on and right away. I had visited the room several times before we dove into clearing it out. My hope was that each time it would get a little easier as I gradually desensitized myself to the shock of what had occurred there. Each time I stood in the doorway, not daring to step inside. I found myself fixated, glaring into that chamber of horror and sobbing in sheer disbelief.

My brother was a true warrior in my eyes on that day when he cleared out and rearranged the attic space. He said it was "no big deal." But I viewed Bill as my knight in shining armor. Because it was frightening to see the exposed rafter where Claude's body had hung just days before, we decided to cover the beam with one of my paintings. I remember feeling exceedingly grateful for his inspiration to do that. It was a perfect solution to replace that gruesome memory with something of beauty. Next, I asked him to suspend a leaded glass crystal in the window of the attic. I was aware of this being a good Feng Shui cure to help clear energy of lower vibrations and activate positive energy. I felt encouraged—this was all a promising beginning.

Eventually, Bill helped me to work up enough nerve to actually step over that threshold. With his support, I was able to walk into the attic rather than holding myself back, standing on the outside looking in. I had to invoke the deepest level of strength from within to do that. I felt my body trembling and my breath constricting, but I was *in*, and I felt proud of myself for being able to achieve that monumental task.

Much to my dismay, I soon after spotted a small clear plastic bag from the local home improvement store resting on top of a storage bin. I had two instantaneous thoughts. First, I suspected that it was the bag that held the rope that Claude used to hang himself. Second, I concluded that the police had overlooked it when they gathered everything relevant to his death during their investigation. My body filled with a rush of heat, and it felt like someone had kicked me in the stomach. I thought *What ... he actually went to the store to buy the rope!?*

Without giving it much thought, I had previously presumed he took it from our garage. To me that would have been less calculated, and more spontaneous, which somehow would have felt less unsettling to me. This confirmed his premeditation to arrive home that day knowing he was going to end his life. Realizing that he had planned this and looking back as I replayed our last phone conversation in my mind from this revised vantage point left me feeling even more outrage.

After a suicide, it's natural for family members to want answers—especially if there is no note. This otherwise unremarkable plastic bag was a piece of that puzzle. I envisioned him walking through the automatic sliding glass doors of the Lowe's we had frequented together. I tried to imagine what it must have been like for him to go in there, proceeding over to the bulk spools of rope and asking an associate to cut the piece that would ultimately drain the life from his body. If only that person knew what Claude had planned for what looked to be an innocuous piece of cord. Was he calm and certain with his resolve, or was he nervous and questioning if he should really do this?

Still raging in the turbulence of my grief, I wanted to solve this mystery. I summoned all of my courage to go to the store, hoping to understand the truth. I felt apprehensive as I made my way through the sliding doors and over to the aisle with the infamous spools of rope. I remember nervously turning the corner, seeing them all in a row hanging well above my head. I just stood there looking up at them, wondering which one he chose, trying to wrap my mind around this new world I was living in. The final confirmation was when I saw the credit card statement. Sure enough, there was a charge for a purchase at Lowe's on the day he died.

The next day, I opened the attic window and burned sage to start clearing the stagnant energy in that room. Then, I lovingly created a circular stone altar on the floor below where he died.

Those stones I used had sentimental value since I had collected them on the beach our townhome had overlooked in Pacifica. It was a beautiful sacred memorial in honor of my beloved Claude. On it, I placed photos, candles, crystals, flowers, and things that were special to him. I had an intuitive insight within the first year that this was simply a portal for his spirit to leave his body—nothing more, nothing less. This alternative perspective proved to be especially helpful and comforting, yet it still took time to tame the impact that that room had on my state of mind. It would always be the place where I experienced the most painful and traumatic event of my life. During the two years we continued living there, I would often feel the urge to go stand in the doorway. It was as if I was staring through a gateway into the past. Though he was gone, on some level, this felt like a connection point to his body and soul. It was the last place that I had physical contact with him.

My art studio was the room just outside of the attic. It wasn't too long before I felt it was time to rearrange and clear the energy in that room so that I could use it to paint again. I felt angry, and it was offensive to think that Claude would kill himself adjacent to a space that he knew I viewed as sacred. I felt some level of violation. The bigger question though, was how he could have done that in our home at all.

I wanted to solve this mystery, too. I sought out intuitive readings, and in one, I was told that Claude felt comforted as he died by being close to a place that I held so dear. It was as if a part of me was with him as he did it. This felt right to me, so I did my best to make peace with his choice and open my heart to knowing that in his mind, I was with him in spirit as he died.

Five days following Claude's death, I met with my team members at our attorney's office. Thankfully, Bill was with me and his calming and reassuring influence helped me cope with that distressing task. Nothing could have prepared me for what I felt when I walked into the room that I had been in countless times as we worked out all the details of our estate planning. None of us could have predicted this unimaginable outcome.

I felt anxious with an unsettled feeling in the pit of my stomach as we were escorted into the conference room by my attorney's assistant.

The team members were positioned around the very same table Claude and I had once sat at together. I felt naked without him by my side. I was now considered a widow in the eyes of the law. My husband was deceased. I would never see him again. Our life together was over. This was now part of my new story, my new normal.

When we walked in, you could have heard a pin drop. As if time had stood still, everyone was silent and looking at me with disbelief and utter despair. Piercing the stillness, Moya, one of the bankers who had worked closely with Claude and his business dealings, sprung up to give me a long and caring hug. I tried, but I couldn't hold back my tears. I felt supported yet exposed and utterly raw in that moment.

The silence in the room persisted as we were shown to the two empty seats. My attorney broke the silence as he led me through all of the steps that needed to be taken care of from a legal standpoint. It was a lot to comprehend in that moment considering the circumstances. In the aftermath of Claude's suicide, I had a safety net for which I was exceedingly grateful. I don't know what I would have done if I hadn't had them there guiding me through the massive swarm of key decisions I was faced with.

Amazingly, I managed to get through the first week accomplishing a great deal with Bill and Leslie's assistance. However, it was time for them to get back to their own lives. Having the two of them with us helped cushion the initial blow of losing Claude. In their absence, I was then left alone to feel the full force and the weight of my grief. It felt like I was moving through mud-wrenched terrain. My momentum slowed considerably. Getting through each moment, each hour, each day became my number one goal. Though all of the details that lay in front of me felt overwhelming, they served an important purpose during that time: They kept me moving forward.

One of those important decisions that ultimately became a personal choice was when to have Claude's memorial service. Since Claude was not religious and wished to be cremated, I had the freedom to hold off on having a service until I could have more time to catch my breath.

I knew Claude wouldn't have wanted a lot of fanfare, so we organized a small gathering by invitation to have his celebration of life ceremony six weeks after his suicide. It was a beautiful heartfelt sharing of music, stories, and memories.

The office space where Claude had his business was an ideal location. The showroom that would normally hold the sample tradeshow exhibits for prospective clients was cleared out and completely transformed by round tables shrouded with white tablecloths. Candles and flowers adorned them in the darkened room creating what felt like a spiritual sanctuary. We catered the event with a nearby favorite Asian restaurant of Claude's. As the service went on, Claude's friends and colleagues stood up and shared their stories of how he had touched their lives, and Noah's friends, Ariana and Natalia, sung an original song accompanied by the violin. To conclude the celebration, I created a full slideshow of our lives together. There wasn't a dry eye among us.

It all went well—so well that I was reassured I had made the right choice when I refused to cave under the pressure I sensed from those who thought I should do it sooner. I had allowed myself the breathing room and the time I needed to develop my resolve and prepare emotionally. As a result, I was able to be more present and appreciate the experience to a greater extent than I would have earlier. This set the tone moving forward for learning and honoring what I needed to take care of myself while I was healing and grieving, regardless of what others may have thought.

I trust that I am safe
& loved
when change arrives at my door.

# 5

# PRESENCE

The prevailing message in our culture is that grief needs to be sequestered, put in a place where nobody can see it. We are not taught as in assorted other cultures how to truly be present with someone who is grieving. Let's face it: We are fearful of death and the dying. Like children, we close our eyes and pretend it doesn't exist. Because of this, we shy away from those who are grieving for fear of our own mortality or of saying or doing something inappropriate.

I have been guilty of this myself. Many years ago on a walk through our neighborhood, I met a woman who told me she had lost her husband. She wasn't much older than me. This may sound absurd, but I remember feeling afraid of her widowhood on some level. I thought if it could happen to her, it could happen to me. This is completely irrational, but I suspect I am not alone in this type of response. Every time I passed her house, I would get this sad and queasy feeling inside. I imagined how hard it must have been for her to be living in the house that they had once shared together. It seemed unimaginable that I would ever have to go through anything like that.

During those first few weeks, I was desperate to talk to anyone who would listen. I was in so much pain that I would grab hold of anyone who came through my front door and just sob in their arms. In hindsight, I'm sure it was a lot for people to handle, but I foolishly thought that they would understand considering what had just happened. After all, they were supposed to be my 'friends,' right? Apparently not. Little did I know that this is one of the normal occurrences when we lose a loved one—people slowly disappear from our lives. One by one, many stopped calling and the visits ended. I often wondered if it was because it was just too much for them, or if they just thought "Well, it's been a few weeks now and she must be over the hump, so we're no longer needed." *WRONG!*

Soon, Noah and I were alone together in our grief—aside from the supernatural occurrences frequenting our home that, when taken as a whole, can't be denied. Claude was unquestionably trying his best to open up a line of communication with me from the other side. Since the circumstances of his death were particularly frightful, I was not too keen on the idea of having him do that. I had been spooked by the whole horrifying experience of finding him. So, I specifically asked him NOT to make himself seen or known in any way, shape, or form.

Unsurprisingly, Claude was steadfast in his determination to make contact. I imagined that he found my resistance rather maddening considering he knew I had the ability to hear and see him. Under different circumstances, I would have welcomed it.

The least intrusive and most loving communication came shortly after he died. I had a lucid dream where he held me securely in his arms. There were no words spoken. I distinctly remember having the awareness in that delicate magical moment that I was in a dream, he was on the other side, and that this was a momentary gift. I desperately held on, knowing that any second this would all fade away.

On many occasions, I felt Claude's presence in the master bathroom over on *his* side, by *his* sink. This seemed to be his custom-built entryway where the veils of separation were most thin. Sometimes I felt comforted by this, and other times it just felt creepy. He would also show up persistently in the kitchen and living room.

The touch light and a touch faucet in our kitchen would erratically turn on by themselves. Instead of feeling scared, I thought it was kind of amusing. Our living room TV seemed to be in cahoots with Claude's parlor tricks as it unexpectedly switched on, interrupting us with loud intrusive chatter at all hours of the day. A little poltergeist action thrown in for the fun of it! Claude did have comedic tendencies after all.

There was another instance when a copy of the movie *The Secret* suddenly slid off the table and onto the floor. Noah and I just looked at each other, eyes wide open. We took that as a clear message that he felt we would be supported in some way by watching it. There were some universal truths presented in the movie that were important for us both to hear as we created a new life after his death, so it felt comforting.

The most significant aspect of this new normal was my responsibility as Noah's mom. I believe that my dedication to upholding this commitment saved my life. With his father gone, my immutable presence was more important than ever. I had to mobilize the energy I needed to get out of bed in the morning to get him to school and carry on with all of my parental duties. It felt daunting considering the impact of my grief—crying, wailing, and screaming had become a part of my daily routine. Since I had listened to the voice that told me to stop screaming and call 911 right away, I was not able to stay with Claude when I found him, which might have helped me release my horror. As a result, it felt crucial to recreate that moment in my mind as many times as I needed to help release the shock and trauma from my body. I hid the worst of it from Noah and I didn't want the neighbors to hear me wailing and screaming, thinking I was in any danger! To remedy this, I set up a scream room in the back of my master closet. I missed Claude to my core and the way he died tormented my very existence.

Claude was a dedicated father and had been steadfast with all of Noah's needs. As a newly-minted single parent, I found it especially challenging to attend school activities without my partner. Seeing intact couples and families was a painful reminder that he was no longer with us. In addition, the finality in the fact that our fourteen-year-old son no longer had his dad was heart-wrenching. It seemed inconceivable that Claude would be absent as Noah began his journey into manhood. Claude would miss seeing him learn to drive, graduate from high school, go off to college, get married, and have children.

Noah and I had different methods of coping and processing our loss. He came to me one afternoon announcing with great confidence and certainty that since his dad was gone, he was now going to "parent himself." I was in shock. I raised my hand and said, "Hello! What about me? I'm still here." He clarified that he would fill the opening that his dad had left vacant. It was a bold and decisive move that I admired him for. I imagine it was his way of taking his own power back and having a sense of control over his destiny. He added that he would set the intention to live a life that his dad would be proud of.

I wasn't sure how to maneuver through this. Yet, I knew full well that my role as his mom was fully intact. We had been tasked with new roles as co-creators building the foundation and framework of our new life without Claude. We would take one step at a time, working our way through what felt like a complex labyrinth with no instructions or preparation on how to navigate this new territory together.

Claude's periodic messages lent us a helping hand on this front. One day, I was in my studio going through a small bin filled with some old papers when I came across three cards that he had given me early on in our relationship. The timing couldn't have been more relevant. Right when I needed his support, there it was. It felt like he was reaching out to me yet again.

On the front of the first one was *"Don't look back!"* with an enchanting illustration of a sign by the side of a forest with an owl perched on top looking down. One sign said *"Your life"* with an arrow going in one direction down one path. The other said *"No longer an option"* with an arrow pointed in the other direction. The delightful character on the card had chosen *Your life* and was happily walking down that path.

Inside he wrote "Hi, just a little inspiration. I love you most of all! C."

This just blew my mind! Could this message have been any more perfect?

There was another card that read *"Life's too mysterious ... don't take it serious!"* With an amusing illustration of a joker pulling his mouth open and sticking his tongue out. Inside Claude had written, "I know you're going through a lot right now. I hope I am able to help turn all this into greatness, Love you, C." Seriously, another whammy!

The third had an image of the famous painting by William Bouguereau called "Ravissement de Psyche." It is a painting of two angels who are clearly in love, one male and one female. He is holding his beloved in full embrace from behind. Claude would frequently come up from behind me and hold me in the same way, so I have always loved this image. Inside it said "We are each of us angels with only one wing ... and we can fly only by embracing each other. I love you, Happy Anniversary." This was yet another magical example of how he was doing his best to send me messages.

Not long after finding the cards, a friend invited me to a local metaphysical fair. I was hesitant to go, since I had been to so many in the past. I really didn't think I would see anything new. Despite that, it felt like there might be something there for me to discover that could be potentially important moving forward. As fate would have it, I met a woman who called herself a Spiritual Rescue Medium. She specialized in connecting with those who have passed and doing energetic house clearings when needed. I liked her and felt certain that she could be of assistance—so much so, that I set up an appointment for her to stop by our home to work her magic.

It seemed as if she could hardly contain herself. Within seconds of her arrival, she revealed that she had been feeling Claude wanting to speak through her. I imagined that he was thrilled to have a channel now, an actual voice to use to speak with me after all those weeks of trying to communicate. She was incredibly spot-on with all that she said about Claude's state of mind before his suicide and what he felt now that he had passed. I wish I had thought to record it since there was so much information pouring through her like a paranormal faucet. It was emotionally intense, and I was in tears the whole time, but it was well worth it. The overriding message was that he was deeply sorry for all of the pain and suffering that he had caused before and after his death. He was not himself when he made that choice to take his life. In addition, he wanted me to know that *it was not my fault*!

Though I knew on some level that it was not my fault and that I truly did everything in my power to help him, it's common to feel guilt when we lose a loved one to suicide. For me it was not the prevalent response, but it was in the mix. This choice that he made to end his life had ignited a wave of grief that in its torturous nature is one of the hardest losses to process. It can haunt loved ones for years with crushing guilt, unyielding heartache, and many unanswered questions.

I was emotionally in disarray, yet somehow, I persevered and found the internal fortitude to do all that was required of me. I would imagine that most people had no idea what I was going through. As time marched on, I became adept at being able to pull it all together while making it look relatively easy. Many told me how impressed they were with how well I was handling things. Looking back, I would have to say that they were right. I rocked it! Thankfully I already had a toolbox filled with things that I had learned from previous losses—the death of both of my parents, divorce, a miscarriage, and the death of pets to name a few. I could draw from those experiences, giving me the strength I needed as I traveled along this path.

Through all of this, I found myself having one recurring anxious thought: With Claude gone, I had lost my primary "love source." I no longer had that "special someone," "my person" to be there loving and supporting me through all of my life experiences. This was a familiar feeling that visited me when each one of my parents died. It was so intense that I felt panic-stricken at times. On a primal level, I felt that my very survival depended on these connections being intact.

But then, spontaneously, an awakening occurred as I was going about my daily tasks. It came to me through my inner guidance that in actuality, Claude was not my primary source of love. That was merely an illusion and a story that I had told myself all those years we were together. In truth, he was just one manifestation of the many ways that love can show up in my life. Since I believe that I am an aspect of God or Source, the true wellspring of love, I also came to realize that such love is ever-present. We are fully supported in the unseen realms by what I would call our angels or guides, including our ancestors or passed loved ones. Because of this, we are truly never alone and never without love. Yes, Claude was still gone from this physical plane, and I was still without my partner, but realizing these higher truths felt comforting to me. It calmed my emotions and helped me feel a greater sense of peace. This was one of the many iridescent pearls of wisdom that would be revealed to me along this journey through grief.

*I am never alone.*

*Love is ever-present.*

*I invite my angels to*

*hold and comfort me.*

# 6

# CHRYSALIS

Summer was rapidly approaching, and I was faced with the undeniable fact that Noah would be going on a school-sponsored trip to the Galapagos Islands. It was the trip of a lifetime that we had all planned together months before Claude's suicide. However, given the unforeseen circumstances, the thought of him going out of the country made me want to take it all back. Having just lost my husband less than two months prior, I didn't have the resilience to handle anything happening to Noah. But it was all set, and I wasn't about to cancel. I knew it would be an extraordinary experience for him.

While we waited at the airport, my heart ached, and I felt that familiar sense of isolation as I saw all of the other parents with their children. It was one more reminder that the part Claude once played in our lives had been forever altered; Noah no longer had a father to share in these significant life moments. Yet even with these triggers, there was excitement and gratitude that he would have this opportunity to travel and see other parts of the world, so I put those feelings aside and lovingly saw him off with an enormous hug and a smile.

While Noah was away, the house felt particularly large and empty, even cavernous. Claude's absence was enhanced by this void. I was grateful to have our two dogs to keep me company, which helped to take the edge off. At the same time, it felt satisfying to have that break from parenting to focus on myself and get ready for our annual summer trip to Asheville, North Carolina, since we would be leaving within a day of Noah's arrival back home. I was especially looking forward to spending time in our tranquil hideaway, knowing it was precisely the medicine we needed.

We named our Asheville home "Sunset Haven," a homage to the stunning sunsets and retreat from the lifestyle in Tennessee that we didn't feel aligned with. For six years, we had owned this property, using it as a vacation rental. In addition, Noah and I always spent several weeks there during the summer months, with Claude typically taking a few weeks off to join us. I had hoped to live there one day, but our lives took an obvious detour with Claude's suicide.

Having this treasured mountain home was a dream come true for me. While I was at Sunset Haven, I felt more at peace and connected to my Divine Self. Floating in a verdant sea of trees and mountains was supremely healing for me, and I had the sense that it would be so again that first summer after Claude died.

With zero contact, Noah's ten-day trip was unquestionably challenging for me, but before I knew it, he was back, safe and sound. I felt a huge sense of relief and joy upon his return, and it was awesome to see his photos and to hear about his travel experiences, especially knowing that this was something that Claude had really wanted for him.

The very next day, we were on the road to Asheville.

Unlike previous years, I felt a bit nervous when we arrived. I wondered how it would feel to be there now that everything had changed. You see, Asheville holds another tender piece of the puzzle for me. It was the place where I spent the last 'normal' week with Claude before his decline and eventual death nine months later.

He'd taken a week off just as in other years. Noah was at camp, so it was just the two of us. It was a special time to reconnect, explore charming little towns in the mountains around Asheville, and dream of the future and the possibilities it held for us. I distinctly remember a foreboding feeling engulfing me as I watched him begin his journey home to Memphis. It felt like things would never be as sweet or as special as they were that summer; it felt like things would never be the same. In that moment, it was impossible to know the magnitude of that precognition.

Once in Asheville, the usual rush of wonder I typically felt upon arrival was tainted by the memories of Claude I confronted everywhere I turned. It was painful. In the evening hours, I felt his absence keenly. That was the time when we would have normally had our daily phone conversations, catching up and telling each other that we loved one another. I sure missed him that first summer!

When the day came to drop off Noah at his favorite camp, the level of support we received upon our arrival heartened me. I let them know ahead of time about Claude so that if anything came up while Noah was there, they would be prepared. With their arms encircling us, the staff assured me that he would be well taken care of during his stay. I left feeling a sense of peace and relief knowing he was in good hands.

With Noah all squared away at camp, the focus was once again back on me. In a peculiar way, Noah's time in the Galapagos had prepared me for what was to come—more time alone. I was in a sense more alone now, hidden away and perched on our secluded mountaintop.

Many fears arose, coming at me in what felt like an onslaught— fear of what the future would hold for me and Noah, and that I would no longer be loved in quite the same way without my beloved Claude alongside me; fear that I would be alone, and that my life would not have the same meaning anymore; fear of how I could possibly create a new life without him, not knowing what that life may look like; fear of giving my heart to another; fear that my heart couldn't face another loss; fear that I didn't have the strength to get through this; fear that I would never live a 'normal' life without grief.

Living in these fears makes for an exceedingly lonely and isolating existence for those of us who are in the throes of grief. Even if we are among others and not actually shut away, our hearts and minds are not truly understood or supported as we move through this most vulnerable time in our lives. What a different world it would be if our culture as a whole could embrace and support those that have suffered a significant loss over the long haul. I learned pretty early on that grief is mostly an inside job, a solo journey. In large part, I needed to retreat from the world with my grief as my new sidekick for better or worse.

Within the silence of my solitude, frightful traumatic memories and flashbacks of finding Claude persisted, streaming through my mind and my heart. Rather than trying to shut them out or numb them with distractions, I confronted each of these fears. Since I was surrounded by a sea of trees and mountains with no other houses in sight, I could scream as much and as loud as I needed to when the unavoidable impulse to purge my feelings arose. What a relief it was to feel the inspiration and the freedom to fully surrender and express the wildness of my emotions completely untamed. Thankfully, as the summer passed, I felt seen, loved, and held in all of my brokenness. I was able to progressively process this loss one layer at a time, one wave at a time, one scream at a time.

Alone in my grief, I found a silver lining. I came to the understanding that there are two faces to our grieving passage: On the one hand, we are shown that we need to go into hiding for fear of judgment due to a lack of understanding. However, as with everything in life, there is a flip side.

On the other hand, there is an important, deeply powerful and transformative element to the alone time that shouldn't be overlooked. We can choose to view our time in the dark moon phase as something sacred and part of the natural part of our life's passage and our souls' evolution. It can be viewed as part of an initiation into the Widow's

Moon, leading us into a deeper connection with our true selves and our changing life purpose.

When we grieve, we are in a state of metamorphosis, just as the butterfly must have its time in its chrysalis. This is an active time, fraught with change, followed by darkness, patience, and struggle. While we grieve, we spend months, or sometimes years, engulfed in the blackness of our own little cocoons, struggling, suffering, processing our feelings, hopefully healing over time, and trying to make sense of it all. It can be a time of deep transformation.

What holds true for the butterfly holds true for us as we grieve. We can't open and emerge from the chrysalis before we are ready. Patience and permission from within are needed to allow this process to unfold naturally. It needs to be experienced in a way that only we can dictate. No one understands our grief the way we do, and nobody can tell us what our journey should look like. Some people may be able to 'move on' as many think we 'should' relatively quickly, and others will grieve for the rest of their lives in one form or another. In other words, there is a broad spectrum of how we participate with and experience our loss over time.

My mission was clear for that summer: I not only needed the contemplative and restorative time that my hideaway would provide, but also to discover my healing path. I had a sense that healing and re-aligning my body, mind, and soul would be the only way I would ever find peace and joy again.

Since painting had become something that felt particularly therapeutic for me, I looked forward to setting up my garage 'pop up' studio. I LOVED painting in Asheville. My van was loaded from top to bottom with all my art supplies each time we went there. I enjoyed painting with the garage door wide open, rain or shine, my music playing in the background. The peaceful and inspirational environment was an ideal setting.

This summer was no different. Painting was definitely in the mix and was an important piece that helped me, as I knew it was part of my life purpose to create paintings that were not only beneficial for me but also for others. With my healing background, it was about creating art that felt soothing, touching us deeply in our souls. Since I no longer had a massage practice, it was another way that I could engage and tap into that universal energy, transmitting this frequency into the paintings. In other words, *having that sense of purpose* was an integral part keeping me moving forward through my grief.

Closed up in my contemplative chrysalis, it wasn't too long before I realized I needed to start looking for some outside assistance with this quest towards healing.

Thankfully, I was clear on where I wanted to begin. I had already been working with Marianne, an amazing modern-day priestess and shamanic energy medicine practitioner. I met Marianne two years before Claude's death. Each summer, I looked forward to reconnecting with her in person after doing remote phone sessions as needed throughout the year. From the first moment we met, there was an instant connection. It felt as if we had known each other before in another time and place. Right away, I felt comfortable with her loving and healing presence.

After my first session, I was profoundly impressed by her intuitive and healing abilities. I had been to many healers over the years, but the purity of her work was unmistakable, filled with unique depth and power. I felt enveloped in the sacred mystical world of the unseen, which was profoundly transformational and restorative. I had found a true medicine woman who could help me reconnect to that part of me that had been put on the shelf after retiring from my massage practice and devoting the majority of my energy to being a mom and a wife. In essence, I knew she could help me remember and awaken more fully to the truth of my divinity. This would prove to be another essential component moving forward.

She had her office at a holistic healing center in nearby Black Mountain. I set up several sessions with her over those six weeks. In addition to working with Marianne, I knew I wanted some bodywork.

She told me about an amazing massage therapist named Michael who worked at the same location. I knew the importance of touch especially after losing my spouse, not to mention the added benefits of stress and anxiety reduction. He sounded like the perfect match for me with his specialty in energy work and hot stone massage. Getting massages was without a doubt going to be a top priority to include in my newly-forming self-care toolkit. Marianne and Michael's work blended flawlessly together. I felt sincere, heartfelt respect and reverence as they each in their own loving way honored the magnitude of my loss, helping to validate its impact.

To further this nourishing and nurturing approach, I attended Marianne's Divine Feminine shamanic circles. In those circles, Marianne led us through sacred ceremonies and energetic shamanic journey work using the breath to reach deep states of consciousness. This in turn allows a deeper connection to the Divine within us, leading us to find answers on our path to healing. I felt supported as I shared my story of what had happened to Claude only three months before. I met some remarkable women who were unconditionally loving towards me at a time when I really needed that. They assured me that I was doing incredibly well considering it was so soon after Claude's suicide. This was critically important for me to hear. I was living in my own vacuum of despair, so it felt invaluable to have an outsider's objective perspective. One woman, Lynn, shared that she kept seeing a large group of angels surrounding our group. After we were done, she came and put her hand on my back by my shoulder blade, saying that she saw a place where a wing would attach. She said it with wholehearted reverence and love; it felt like a message from those angels who were there holding space with us. This was the beginning of my development of a more genuine understanding of the role my angels were playing in my life and of the angelic origins of my soul.

It wasn't long before the effects of working in the shamanic domain began spilling over within plain sight of our 3-D world. A wonderful example of how this manifested was during an encounter with a spirit animal one night while Noah was still at camp. Deep in thought as I typed away at my computer, I was startled by a loud thud behind me, breaking my concentration. It sounded like a bird had flown into the double glass door that led outside to the wraparound deck. I paused to consider how odd that would be given it was nighttime. Fortunately, the outdoor porch light enabled me to see that there was a very small owl sitting on the deck. Its vast penetrating eyes gazed into my soul for what felt like an eternity. It was an awe-inspiring, mystical moment. I kept eye contact as I slowly lowered myself onto the floor, gradually sliding closer. I was breathless as I had no idea how much time we would have together. This instance of fleeting impermanence took me back to the dream I had after Claude died, when he held me in his arms. This sweet owl and I were held by the stillness for just a few moments with our eyes fixated on one another. Then, as quickly as she came, she flew away. I marveled at this encounter and puzzled over what the message was. Not too long after settling back into my computer world, there it was again, another loud thud against the glass door. Yup, it was my little owl friend. Not once, but twice, seemed like an even more potent engagement. It felt like a gift from Spirit helping me see past the illusion of separation and reminding me once again that I was loved and never alone.

As humans, we can sometimes be afraid of the darkness, the unseen, or the unknown. Owls thrive in that world. The owl is a symbol for clairvoyance, being able to see what many others cannot. The owl's medicine that night evoked the message that I could access my inner wisdom and intuition, helping me to find my new direction, my new true north. I told my sister about it days later and her immediate response was "I think it was Claude." I have heard many stories about visitations from loved ones who have passed showing up as butterflies, animals, and birds, etc. I would never know for sure if that was indeed Claude, but it was a symbolic encounter that made me stop and ponder my reality and the thin veil that exists between our worlds.

Yet it was only with my healing practitioners that I was able to be completely candid. Otherwise, I learned that in order to have a somewhat 'normal' life, putting on a happy face and pretending that everything is OK was the way to go. I got the message that most people didn't want to hear how I was *really* doing. The truth can be too much for people to fathom. On top of that, I was fearful of losing even more friends from my life, so I generally shared half-truths. I didn't tell others how desperate I felt inside. I didn't tell them how I wondered if I would ever move through this grief and devastation.

The other motivating factor to wearing the *"all is well"* mask was my need to enjoy the present moment and being with others. It was a welcome oasis and distraction from my seemingly endless suffering. It was a break from the overwhelming thoughts and feelings that haunted me while I was alone. It felt good to get out of my own madness and be able to listen to other people's stories and experiences. But make no mistake—once the social time was up, it was right back to my grief.

Even with all of the healing work helping me tremendously, I was beginning to feel doomed to what seemed like a life sentence in the prison of grief. But I came to learn that grief does not have a final destination. With this new insight, I began seeing that if you can imagine even a small fracture through the darkness of your grief and have a desire to heal and find your own renewed purpose, there is light at the end of the tunnel. It does not mean your pain will go away—it won't. But it will temper with time. Yes, it's true, your life will never be the same. But over time, it is possible to emerge from your own chrysalis as someone who is stronger and ready to engage with the world in a way that you never could have imagined.

There is no right or wrong here. For me, recognizing that this experience could serve as an opportunity for healing and creating a new life was coming into focus. I came to realize that this road is unavoidably imbued with ups and downs. Healing takes time, along with a lot of strength, tenacity, determination, and most importantly, commitment. I came to realize that I would have to commit myself to repeatedly weathering this storm in one piece. I wanted to heal my tattered heart.

Looking back on that time, I followed the wisdom of my soul, guiding me as I created the perfect recipe to assist me with that first stage of my healing. The combination of being in Asheville and the team that I had chosen to support me while I was there all helped me feel more empowered moving into the next chapter of my grieving and restorative process. The task of healing myself felt massive, but I knew I was well on my way, having gotten what I needed from these amazing practitioners and women that crossed my path.

Just as the butterfly needs to struggle to emerge from the protection of its chrysalis, so do we need that process that can lead us to a place where we can one day fly. I was still in my chrysalis that summer in our Asheville home, without any thought of trying to rush the process. There can be no forcing grief to be something it isn't ready to be.

*I surrender my sorrow to*
*Mother Earth,*
*knowing she embraces me as*
*I walk this path of heart-healing.*

# 7

# CLARITY

Feeling fatigued after a long day's drive from North Carolina, Noah and I began the arduous task of unpacking the van. We walked into the kitchen from the garage, our bags in hand, which harkened back to that fateful day just four months before when Claude took his life. There was an eerie similarity in the way energy in the house felt—vacant and soulless. I noticed my body tightening and my breath starting to constrict. Any sense of peace that I had cultivated after spending six weeks in my enchanting mountain retreat was beginning to dissipate.

Re-entry was typically hard on me even in the best of times. I would invariably feel mixed about being back, renewed yet saddened to be leaving it all behind until our next scheduled visit. Just as I had anticipated, this year was particularly challenging and complex. Claude wasn't there to temper the upset or greet us with his loving, open arms as he had been every other summer. Not only that, I was once again physically face-to-face with the harsh reality of Claude's suicide within the confines of our home. While away, I'd had the opportunity to distance myself from that brutal truth, but now there was no getting around it. That room where I found him existed; it really did happen.

Nevertheless, I arrived home with an unwavering resolve to free myself from the aftermath of an undeniable event that had embedded itself into my psyche. Over the course of those first few months, one thing that had become apparent to me was the fundamental power of choice and the impact my choices would have on my overall well-being moving forward. I alone had the power to choose how I would traverse this unexplored terrain through grief.

I saw myself at a crossroads with the likelihood of living in one of two conceivable scenarios.

Option one: I could settle on a way of life frozen in emotional collapse and filled with fear, despair, anger, pessimism, and sorrow— void of any hope or meaning.

Option two: I could seek the healing of my heart, leading to the gradual unfolding of my revitalized life path and purpose. I could allow myself to rise up and find my wings to fly again, renewed and recalibrated.

I knew it wouldn't be easy; however, option two was by far the more appealing and obvious choice for me. I knew I wanted to heal and find my way through this with the best possible approach. With this as my intention, it was evident that I needed a broader team of support who would hold my hand as I walked on this precarious path. The hope was that each gifted wayshower would provide me with a safety net permitting me to go into the depths of my grief where true healing and transformation could occur as I held the light and dark as one.

Before we knew it, summer break was over, mid-August was upon us, and Noah's school was back in session. With that transition behind us, I could reactivate my grief tending. The healing work I did over the summer laid a sound foundation, yet what I had gained felt fragile and tenuous. I needed to shore it up with further reinforcements to keep my forward momentum intact. The timing couldn't have been more favorable to begin phase two of my healing journey.

At first, the task before me felt daunting, considering the level of grief I was still experiencing. I wasn't sure where to begin. However, one thing I knew with certainty was the healing power of nature and the important role that played in my life. With this awareness, I made the commitment to continue with my daily walks. Getting outside each day kept my body moving, which in turn helped me feel that I was moving forward one baby step at a time.

Sitting in the forest or on a mountain top always helps me to feel grounded and calms my nervous system. One day, amongst the towering trees, I asked for guidance and support from my angels. This is a practice that I have grown accustomed to as I believe we each have a spirit posse of sorts. We are surrounded by an ever-present group of angelic guardians or guides that are here with us from birth to look after us through all of life's challenges. It is much like a prayer when I call on them to receive insights into a situation where I may need their assistance. This, in turn, can help me see what direction or actions to take. Sometimes, it simply helps me remember the truth of who I am as a divine being beyond my pain and suffering.

On that particular day, as I asked them to lend me their loving support, I heard this message:

> *Standing tall in who we are, remembering the power of Spirit coursing through us at every moment—this is where we find our strength. This is where we find our resolve. This is where we find our peace. Through it all, we remember, we remember.*

> *We are asked to stand in our grief but usually not feeling so tall as we do so. When we can rise up to remember our soul's journey through all of these chaotic emotions, we can find our salvation, even if only for a moment. With time, these moments become hours, become days, become months. This can help us find perspective and understanding through this journey called life.*

There is an invitation to stillness in the serenity that nature provides. When we are able to 'just be,' we open the doors a little wider, listening to the depth of our soul and our own inner wisdom. The more we can unlock our resistance and learn from these messages, the more we can start to acknowledge that we are always being guided. Our higher consciousness can act as a beacon directing our awareness and understanding as we move through our grief and our lives.

Having the knowledge that there is always a bigger picture at play in the divine scheme of things is another important piece of the puzzle for me, putting things in the greater context of our human existence. In any given experience, even one that feels unreal and beyond the scope of our imagining, our souls have our backs. We are always being watched over and taken care of. We simply need to ask for help along the way and radically trust that we are being cared for at every turn.

My nature practice was a good beginning, but my quest continued. Toward the end of August, I sought help from a therapist who I had known for years, Catherine. She held a unique position from all the others in that she knew Claude personally, having spent many hours with us during our couple's counseling sessions. Because of that, she was an invaluable shoulder to cry on. However, within a month, I felt a need to find someone who specialized in grief counseling. Soon, I discovered that a local hospice center offered free grief support. I found this to be reassuring; nevertheless, making that phone call felt like another massive hurdle I needed to jump over. It was further admission that Claude was truly gone and that yes, he took his own life.

Paige became my grief counselor. After the initial phone interview, I scheduled an appointment and continued with the individual grief counseling for almost two years. I imagined that talking with her, I would feel a sense of liberation in revealing how he died without watering it down. It seemed reasonable to expect that she had heard it all through her years of experience with helping others through grief. As it turned out, I was right. She provided the safe space I needed to express all the gory details and emotions that I held back from others for fear of burdening and alienating them. She gave me the emotional support I craved in addition to bearing witness to my torturous and complex journey as a suicide survivor.

She helped me to know with certainty that I was not going crazy; at times, it really felt that way. In addition, I gained a deeper understanding of what it means to *really* allow oneself to grieve: To allow ourselves the freedom to surrender or lean into our grief rather than turning away. Among other things, I learned that each one of us will have our own unique way of experiencing or moving through grief—that there is no right or wrong, and that grief is messy and has its own individual timeline and trajectory. This was all exceedingly valuable and illuminating, particularly at the early stages of my grieving process.

Integrating the work of both Paige and Catherine was a godsend. However, I wanted to work at an even deeper soul level. So, in addition to the more traditional methodology of psychotherapy and grief counseling, I chose to expand on that to include a more holistic spirit-centered approach to healing, something that I had already begun in Asheville with the help of Marianne and Michael.

Once back in Tennessee, I still had the option of working with Marianne remotely, but I hoped to find some additional practitioners that I could see in person. Knowing how much I benefited from the transformative breathwork with Marianne over the summer, I made an appointment with Daniel. I had taken meditation classes with him in previous years and discovered that he also did private breathwork sessions. The session I had with him was certainly beneficial, but intuitively I felt I needed something different moving forward. In actuality, I believe the true reason I was divinely guided to see him was to find out about Gwen. After my session with him, I saw a stack of business cards resting on the table beside me. There was an energetic radiance around them that made me want to learn more. As he described her work, I noticed how drawn I was to this approach. Later that day, I looked at Gwen's website. Her distinctive heart-centered energy and the love that she embodies were evident. I was excited to have this opportunity and couldn't wait to meet her.

Gwen is a spiritual teacher, master energy healer, hypnotherapist, sound healer, intuitive guide, and life coach. She greeted me on a cool October day with an abundance of love and compassion. I immediately felt safe. With her intuitive insights and angelic presence, I knew right away that she was a gifted healer, her work carrying the highest level of integrity. It felt like a perfect fit, and I knew I had found my teacher and guide to help me gain deeper understanding of Claude's suicide and the role that was playing in my life.

I liked her so much that I wondered if Noah might want to give her a try. All things considered, Noah was functioning well with school and friendships but was suffering from some degree of depression. He wasn't interested in doing grief counseling, but when I told him about Gwen, it was like a light bulb went off inside. He was intrigued by her metaphysical slant and wanted to explore that domain. Much to my chagrin, my spiritual beliefs had not influenced him at all as he matured. He, like Claude, was more of an agnostic at that point in his young life. Working with Gwen would be an opportunity to explore and gain understanding about his True Self and his soul's innate wisdom, opening him to a whole new world filled with previously unfamiliar concepts and teachings. His curiosity level was high, and he wanted to be shown or proven that this world of the unseen does, in fact, exist. I suspected, too, that he was looking for answers and insights into his father's suicide and how that event and his experience of that fit into the grand scheme of his life.

It didn't take long for Gwen's work to win us both over. She reinforced that we have the inner ability to heal our wounds with our thoughts and intentions. Month after month, we worked with her on releasing outdated beliefs, patterns, and programs from our past. We were grateful to have her show up in our lives just when we needed her most. With Gwen holding our hands, we were held in love and light as we gradually found our way through the ravages of grief.

She illuminated our journey and guided us to a deeper place of self-awareness and self-love. Through her intuitive work, I learned that Claude was now on his own journey and that he was with us in spirit, loving and guiding us from the other side. It felt comforting to know that. From a more spiritual perspective, she helped me gain clarity on his suicide. This helped set me free from the responsibility and guilt that I carried for his personal decision to take his own life. Over time, she would become an invaluable friend, advisor, and mentor to us both as we explored this new way of life without Claude.

Meeting Gwen led us to Betty. This turned out to be a package deal. Gwen traveled to Memphis from her home in Nashville to see clients one week per month, and it just so happened that Betty was Gwen's host for her stay in Memphis. Once we got into our monthly appointment groove with Gwen, it was a natural progression for both Noah and me to explore and experience Betty's work, since they were both in the same location.

Betty is another gifted massage therapist who also does various types of energetic transformational work. I sought her services as another loving, nurturing presence in my life. With each month that passed after Claude's suicide, my desire for touch grew ever more present. Of course, it wasn't the same kind of tender caress you receive from a loving partner, but it nonetheless felt heavenly to have that comforting, soothing contact. The universal healing energy streaming through her hands helped me feel an even greater sense of the peace and calm that I so desperately needed.

I felt assured knowing that my healing support team was now fully in place. Each one in their own unique way helped to put me back together again piece by piece like Humpty Dumpty after this unimaginable fall into the kingdom of grief.

Meanwhile, as I was busy putting my team of invaluable healers in place, I had another team working in the background on the complex, unresolved issue of selling the business that Claude had been running for the final thirteen years of his life.

To Claude's credit, he had laid out a plan for me to activate in the event of the unthinkable, which meant I had a group of people to turn to. Had he not carefully chosen and assembled them to assist me, I would have been lost in a sea of despair and uncertainty. I couldn't have asked for a more capable crew on board to help with this formidable task.

Despite this, I imagined having conversations with Claude about that whole torturous experience many times. Even though I had the help I needed to sell the business, I was exceedingly angry that I had to deal with it at all. I was struggling to stay on track each day with the basics, never mind dealing with this monumental undertaking. It was stressful and agonizing, full of emotional triggers. He had put so much of his vital force into the business, and in some ways, that may have contributed to his death. In the end, though, I was in a place of gratitude and felt a tremendous sense of relief to have that burdensome ordeal behind me when the sale went through in the fall of that first year.

As a result of working with my healing team, I started to recognize that grief had a purpose beyond just making me feel trapped in an unimaginable web of despair and isolation. With this insight, I knew that I needed to shift my perspective. Yes, it's true that grief has taken me to unbearable depths emotionally, but its purpose was not to break me. The purpose of my grief has been to take me on a spiritual journey of growth and rebirth. Grief has been my teacher leading me far down the rabbit hole on a mission that would inevitably crack me wide open, revealing the light within and ultimately, the truth of my own divinity. The more I have been able to lean into my experience of grief, the more I have viewed this as an odyssey imbued with wisdom and untold gifts.

*I love myself through the tears.*
*My tears are the song of my heart,*
*I freely let them sing.*

# 8

# SURRENDER

Knowing that I have faced this unimaginable loss, one might assume that feeling any sense of gratitude would be elusive or unattainable. However, as I review all that I have been through, I can say with certainty that gratitude is alive and well, living alongside my grief. In fact, gratitude is one of the most valuable tools and greatest gifts to put into practice as we move through our grief. When we are able to create a bridge from grief to gratitude, we open a doorway to an elevated level of understanding. With this refreshed perspective, we can't help but reframe our thoughts. This brings us into the present moment where true healing may occur. As a result, we are no longer stuck in the seemingly endless loop of despair. We can instead bring our attention to the many blessings that encapsulate our lives. Gratitude has become an integral part of my journey. Without it, I would be lost in my grief with no hope of finding the light. In saying this, I do not mean to suggest that gratitude overshadows or can take away our pain. However, it can relieve some of the suffering that walks hand-in-hand with grief.

In order to truly grow and evolve from this experience, I have had to be courageous and become a grief warrioress—not with the intention of going into battle with grief but of yielding completely to its transformative nature. I must say yes to uncovering the mysteries and the brilliant jewels that grief wields. As I take each step along this path of breadcrumbs, I am watchful of signs and symbols that present themselves, maintaining the awareness that there are many avenues on which we can receive spiritual guidance and direction.

I knew it was up to me to be willing to listen and tune in as things were evolving and, in due course, coming into form. This is where deepening my level of trust in my intuition and inner guidance system became most important. Thankfully, I had already been listening to my higher wisdom, but things were accelerating during this season of grief. I needed continued support from my healing team to keep me afloat as I sought validation and reassurance that I was on track with my intuitive insights. Over time, this collaboration would become invaluable.

One of the common threads that has been ceaselessly reaffirmed is that we are, in our essence, radiant and divine beings living a human experience of our own design. While we are here on planet Earth, we have agreed to undergo an abundance of circumstances. Some might call it our 'soul's curriculum.' The curriculum that we as individuals signed up for holds the template for how our lives will unfold and the life experiences that we draw to us. Each one of these experiences is designed for our soul's growth and spiritual evolution. With this knowledge, even grief can be viewed as a blessing.

Despite this view of our human condition, I faced a persistent urge to resist. The struggle and pain that I felt my grief inflicted were exhausting. In other words, I just wanted it to be *over*. Who wouldn't!? It was during one of those periods that I was gifted with this piece of insightful wisdom from my angelic guides, which perfectly illustrates my view on the strength and the value of surrender as we move through grief:

> *Let's imagine for a moment, if you can, that this is a deep dive into the pool of surrender. We need to give ourselves over to this*

*experience fully and completely. It is what our souls require. The soul will accept no less than our complete and total commitment to allowing grief to have its way with us. If you can allow complete surrender to the pain, trusting that you will come out the other side in one piece, you will discover the true gifts that grief can give you. What you find is up to you. It will vary by person, but one thing is for sure: you will come out anew. The waves of emotions will tumble all the rough surfaces into a smooth, flowing, beautiful stone that can be taken with you as YOU!*

*If you can allow yourself to begin to look at the big picture, what you will find is that it is ALL perfect and in direct alignment with Spirit and your soul's divine blueprint. From where you stand right now, it may not seem that way. You may be in total darkness and despair, but that, too, is part of this journey. You can't have the light without the dark. They exist side by side— they are one. You will have many opportunities to dwell in both as you pass through this human experience. Allow each to have its way with you; all things must pass, one flowing into the other. So, take heart when you are in the depths of despair, seeing no way out. Just wait and be patient; this too shall pass and cycle into joy once more.*

With purposeful practice, I have incorporated the belief that we are much more than our personality, small self, or ego self—that we are always in alignment with all that occurs in our lives, even when it does not look or feel that way. We are continuously given opportunities for growth without fully comprehending the magnitude of the gifts that our Divine or Higher Selves are presenting to us in each of these opportune moments. In the end, everything and everyone serves a higher purpose on this trek we call life. I am grateful for these enlightened perspectives that have carried me through my darkest hours, illuminating my path through this most heart-wrenching experience.

Throughout my grieving and healing odyssey, I have gained wisdom and knowledge far beyond what I would have comprehended if Claude had not left this life. I am grateful for my ever-deepening relationships with trust, love, acceptance, surrender, understanding, self-love, gratitude, intuition, truth, forgiveness, freedom, transformation, oneness, courage, purpose, strength, wisdom, presence, compassion, creativity, divine order, flow, and joy. Simply put, I am living my life with greater intention, and my relationships with my Self and with others are imbued with a more expansive level of awareness and consciousness than they were in the past.

Through all the seasonal changes, I kept up with my morning walks—or mourning walks as I liked to call them—in nature. Tears would often accompany me, especially during the first several months when I was at the peak of emotional turmoil. I sometimes felt complete and utter desperation breaking with the weight of the pain I carried. One day, I chose a tree (or maybe the tree chose me) to lean into for support. Thanks to the tree's steady and majestic spirit, this communion felt like a calm in the storm. I asked the impressively tall tree with all its wisdom to ground my relentless agony through its roots into Mother Earth, helping to relieve some of the burden of the despair I carried. In time, I could feel its wondrous aura embracing me each time I visited. This became a cherished place for me to release my tangled emotions, a small sanctum of comfort as I processed my loss.

I received countless insights on these walks. One day while I was out with my two little white poodles experiencing a profound sense of grief, I saw a woman in the distance jogging toward me. In the moment when she approached, I recognized her as someone that I'd met on that same trail maybe a year before. Right away, I observed how effortless her gait was, as if she were floating on air. I noticed, too, that she was beaming with a huge smile that filled her face to the brim. She was captivating as she appeared before me, embodying the qualities of an angel or vison from God. Then, all of a sudden, it dawned on me—the icing on the cake of this scene. I remembered her name was Joy!

This jolted me out of my oblivious grieving state. I felt that there were two messages delivered by the Universe for my consideration. The first was that joy and grief can exist side by side. We can choose which stream of consciousness we align ourselves to in any given moment. The second is that joy was not only possible for me to experience again, but it was also manifesting right before my eyes.

With these insights, I knew that, with patience, I would get through this expanse of grief and that joy was within my reach. It was comforting to become aware of my authority to choose my inner monologue and that my grief would not always have dominion over me. This reinforced that I have the ability to change my perspective at any given moment, which in turn helped me to feel more empowered. I became more conscious of my part in the creation of the world I was inhabiting, internal and external.

This is not to say that I would turn my back on grief, since I knew the importance of embracing it. However, with this new revelation, I could now adjust my orientation to it should I choose to. Simply taking a break in those moments when I embraced my own joy became a brief refuge. Over time, those intervals of joy would naturally increase.

These walks became a haven of transmissions from the unseen world. One might say that I was receiving communication from Claude or perhaps my Higher Self, spirit guides, angels, or nature spirits. These allegorical dispatches would show up in the form of repeated sightings of deer, butterflies, cardinals, hawks, and snakes, along with blue heron, owl, and hawk feathers to name a few. Each of these sacred symbols came with a distinct meaning and message. Deer often showed up to remind me to be extra loving and gentle with myself; snakes reassured me that I was living in a time of transmutation and spiritual transformation; and hawk medicine signaled the wisdom of viewing my situation from a higher perspective and trusting my intuition. I cherished these signals, knowing that I was being guided and supported through the darkest moments of my grief.

Since these had been recurring encounters as I moved through all of the moon phases, I felt comforted and was learning to trust that I was not alone even when I felt most vulnerable and downhearted. I learned that they can serve as beacons directing my awareness and understanding. It was through this natural world that my connection to Spirit continued to be awakened, and in turn, my connection to Self was emerging in a new and deeper way.

It was late winter when Gwen introduced me to the work of Paul Selig's channeled texts. I devoured the first two books, reading them multiple times. If you could see my copies, you might laugh. You would find that they are filled cover to cover with underlines, highlighted passages, earmarked pages, and sticky notes spilling from the outer edges of the books.

The teachings of 'The Guides' in Paul's books are filled with illuminating instruction about our soul's journey in this human experience. I discovered them at just the right moment in time, and their impact has been pivotal. It wasn't so much that the information was entirely new since they reinforced what I had been learning from Gwen and the others on my healing team. But reading his texts brought it all into sharper focus and laid out a framework that I hadn't previously encountered. It felt like the complete package for personal and spiritual growth and knowledge of myself as One with the creator. In other words, they genuinely spoke to me in a language that felt true, resonating on a deep level. To this day, they have been supportive in creating a new vibrational alignment with Self through my grieving process.

Apparently, while reading these books, we are receiving the energetic transmissions from the guides who Paul channels. The books and Paul's workshops have reinforced my approach to life from the position of my omnipresent, Divine Self. For me, this has been one of the most essential ingredients of this Widow's Moon, serving as another of the varied reminders that *I am much more than my human experience of grief.*

I fully acknowledge that there is an abundance of pathways for gaining clarity and perspective through our life's challenges. This is merely one of my personal methodologies for embracing and remembering the ultimate truth of who I am.

Close to the time when Gwen encouraged me to buy Paul Selig's books, Paige told me about a weekly grief support group that was being offered by the hospice center. Since it seemed that it might be supportive to be with others who had had a recent loss, I gave it a try. However, the group was composed of people who had suffered a wide variety of losses. After attending a few sessions, it quickly became apparent that what I really needed was to be with women who had lost their husbands specifically to suicide. I found myself feeling even more cordoned off by my category of loss. I thought at the time that none of the others in my group could possibly comprehend what I had been through, since losing a loved one to suicide is a species unto itself. I imagined that if I could connect with others who understood that exact situation, I wouldn't feel so alone, enduring that unabating weight in utter isolation. Another thing I realized was that I needed to talk with those who could relate to the traumatic experience of finding him—confronting his disfigured body, what that felt like, and the impact it has had on me. I longed to be with other people who had the capacity to fully grasp that soul-shattering experience. This piece for me has been one of the most challenging aspects of my journey, as well as the aspect that has made me feel so set apart. Despite this realization, I stuck with it, learning what I could about grief practices and methods to process my loss.

In that same group, I met a lovely woman who had lost her husband to cancer. Since we had both lost a spouse, we gravitated to one another and typically stayed to talk further after the others had left. One day, after hearing about what she had been struggling with in her grieving process, I felt a strong inner pull to share an insight that I had received the previous week. I thought that if I had found it helpful, then maybe it would prove to be beneficial for her.

My inner guidance has the funny habit of delivering information while I am doing my daily tasks such as taking a shower, folding laundry, etc. One day, while I was washing the dishes, it came to me that our pain and suffering is really about holding on to the past—holding on to what was and will never be again in this timeframe of existence. Simply put, our attachment to a previous reality is the source of much of our suffering. While we are grieving, we have the tendency to rewind and replay images of our loved ones in our mind's eye. We become enchanted by these bygone images. I know I did this with Claude for months after he died. I have since found out that this insight is not exactly original; it's actually a universal truth. But in that moment when it came to me, it felt life-altering and unique. I remember feeling a bit nervous to actually speak the words to this woman. I thought, *What if she takes offense to what I say?*

Nonetheless, I found myself sharing my insight as part of my own journey. I didn't tell her all of this—but I did share my thoughts on our tendency to replay our memories of the past.

*In grief, we are miners digging for gold, finding all of the gems that we have kept hidden from others, and yes, even ourselves. Grieving holds an opportunity—if we allow it—for our soul's purpose to become activated, bubbling to the surface, illuminated in ways that would not have been possible otherwise. This experience has been designed on a soul level. It serves as a catalyst to propel us into this new existence, this new way of perceiving the world and our place in it.*

*The memories play and replay. In desperation, we hold on to every small detail, keeping us from engaging with the sweetness that only the present moment can offer. We can easily get lost in this memory mining. While it can be comforting at times, we can also become enchanted with this search for connection to our loved ones through the pictures in our minds. It's as if by doing this, we believe we are somehow bringing them back to life. But then we snap out of it and realize they are gone, never to return. We are left with that painful realization, leaving us with a gaping hole so big we feel desperate to fill it. So, we keep the memory replay on automatic pilot, hoping that somehow, we can refill that empty space with each installment.*

*But there is an alternative. We can embrace our loss. We can allow it to form and shape us. This is difficult; it requires that we let go of all that we thought we were. We realize we cannot go back. Holding on to the past only brings us pain and suffering, but our salvation is in the present. The longing for what WAS only keeps us stuck and frozen in the immutable hands of time.*

*Here's the secret: when we can break the cycle of our incessant memory replays, then we are truly free to be present in this moment. We can grieve without the suffering. We have more space to breathe and more space to create our new reality, our new life. We are not stuck in the past. We are alive, and we are free, just where our beloved ones want us to be.*

As it turned out, she found it valuable and really took it to heart. She made a point to tell me repeatedly over the next few weeks how much it had helped her with her grief. I was grateful I'd had the courage to open up to her. This was the first time I shared my own personal inner guidance in relation to what I was learning about my own grieving process with a fellow griever. It reassured me that I could have a positive impact and help her through this most painful and difficult time in her life.

Looking back, this was a key moment for me. I was stepping onto a path that I would not fully understand for years to come—a path towards becoming a teacher and writer, sharing my insights and inner guidance as I have journeyed on this path through grief.

In this moment,
I am grateful, & I lean into
the many gifts of my grief.

# 9

# COURAGE

>>>•◦◦◦

Despite all of the energetic clearings, my home art studio never regained its sacred sparkle after Claude died. Although these efforts lessened my unease enough that I was able to continue painting, my work was never really the same. I could see that the energy in the paintings was not as clean and fresh as it had once been. I had to face it—*I* wasn't the same. I was still grieving. Pre-suicide, it was easier for me to surrender myself to the universal current, allowing the bright, abstract, undulating fields of color and light to flow through me. But I was in a different place emotionally, and I was still finding my way through the darkness of grief. Because of this, the vibrancy in my work seemed less clear and more muddled. My paintings during that first year reflected that inner shift, pure and simple.

Before long, the autumnal emergence signaled yet another external transition with its transmuting colors. I noticed an internal redirection in my life purposefully coinciding with this seasonal crossing. My creative center felt like it was being called in another direction. I didn't feel that same pull to paint for others. It felt like a time to paint just for me. In fact, I thought that perhaps I would be better served by diving further into a form of painting that I had discovered years before: Intuitive Process Painting.

It just so happened that the year before Claude's suicide, I had fulfilled my dream to explore this approach by attending a week-long retreat in Taos, New Mexico and studying with Michele Casou, the creator of Intuitive Process Painting. I liked it so much that I had signed up for the next year's workshop right after my first one! My plan to return in the fall had been arranged months before Claude passed. The idea was to meet up with a woman who I had gotten to know during that last workshop, Micki. Upon meeting, we had an immediate connection, and we had stayed in touch via email. She was one of the few people who knew what I was dealing with during that period while Claude was slowly slipping away. She was a trauma therapist, and I appreciated her wisdom, compassionate support, and guidance, which were invaluable during the months leading up to and just after his suicide.

As it turned out, though, another unfortunate change was thrown into the mix that would underscore the theme of my redesigned life—a life now filled to the brim with opportunities for resilience and adaptation. Micki had undergone hip replacement surgery a few weeks before the workshop and was having issues with her recovery. In the end, she was not able to join me there.

I was deeply disappointed and saddened. We had been looking forward to that reunion and the companionship we had both enjoyed so much the year before. Since she helped me through the difficult passage leading up to Claude's suicide, I imagined it would feel comforting to spend time with her in person. Now, the thought of being there without her loving presence made me feel frightened and vulnerable. I questioned my own commitment to going. Despite this, and after careful consideration, I decided to stick with my original intention and attend without her. After all that had transpired with Claude, this trip felt like it would be an important component in working with my grief.

Noah and our two little dogs stayed with Claude's mom, Eleanor. Though I knew without a doubt that Noah felt completely secure with my departure and was in good hands, leaving him behind for ten days felt unsettling. His trip to the Galapagos and his summer camps prepared me on some level, but this felt different. As Noah's only living parent, I found myself worrying, *What if anything were to happen to me on this trip?* Even with these thoughts, I made the decision to trust my inner guidance, having faith that all would be well. Because I was still able to go, it was a relief to step back from all of the obligations, giving myself over to my healing process just as I was able to do in Asheville two months before. I knew how incredibly fortunate I was and felt grateful that I would have this slice of time just for me.

Intuitive Process Painting is a form of self-expression that incorporates tapping into the freedom we feel as children when we make art. While immersed in this technique, we are not concerned with outcomes or with using the 'correct' color or shape. We just go for it, allowing vibrant and spirited images to come through us in the moment as we are faced with that blank piece of paper. It sounds easy, yet as adults, it can be challenging to let go of the conditioning and negative self-talk that most of us have been giving safe haven to for decades.

I thought that the workshop would be an ideal opportunity to invite the freedom of expression during this transformative Widow's Moon. While driving through the breathtaking beauty of the high desert, I realized that New Mexico held some bittersweet emotions. It was strange to think that I had moved to Santa Fe from New Hampshire with my first husband twenty-seven years earlier to go to massage school. I had then moved to San Francisco five years later, leaving Santa Fe as a divorced woman. Now, on this occasion, I was once again without a husband, but under entirely different circumstances.

My surroundings were familiar, and although I was filled with anticipation, I no longer felt the same connection to the state that I'd previously had the good fortune to call home. The life I once shared with my ex-husband, John, felt like a dream ... like another lifetime entirely.

As if that wasn't enough, I came to grips with the realization that the two men I had loved and trusted the most in my life both broke my heart in surprising and unimaginable ways. Though my divorce at age thirty was the most painful event of my life up until that point, in hindsight, I could see that its higher purpose was to redirect my life's path. At age fifty-four, Claude's suicide brought a magnitude of pain that I had never imagined possible. But that, too, has served to alter my life and my soul's evolution in favorable ways that I could never have foreseen at the time of his death.

As I sifted through these thoughts and feelings, I knew I was exactly where I was supposed to be. The timing couldn't have been more opportune. My appreciation for the magical and mysterious allure of the Land of Enchantment had always touched me deeply in my soul. Because of this, I looked forward to receiving the bounty of the earth's healing energy that the New Mexico landscape exudes. It seemed to have all fallen into place as if it were a precisely patterned puzzle piece fitting in to the arrangement of this divine plan. I felt like I was on a pilgrimage to reclaim parts of myself that had been scattered to the wind with these losses.

I was gradually learning that when we are met with a major loss, our souls at the helm, we are taken on the ride of our lives. We will have many opportunities to empower and surprise ourselves as we journey through grief.

I arrived a day early to settle into my accommodations, which were within walking distance to the historic Mabel Luhan House, where the workshop was being held. Typically, workshop attendees stay at the lodge, but being a classic introvert, I wanted to have a private space to decompress in after a long day surrounded by others. Since I was there in advance, I was able to go to the painting studio to scout out and reserve the exact spot where I envisioned spending the next seven days painting. Doing this helped me take care of the scared one inside who felt raw and exposed.

I sent an email to Michele ahead of time, letting her know about my loss so that she would be aware of my situation. Her response was one of caring and support. I felt relieved to know that I would be in nurturing hands throughout the entire workshop.

After warming up on two "easy" paintings over the first few days, I resolved myself to attempt something that I knew would be exceptionally painful and challenging: fulfilling an indelible impulse to paint an image of my horrific experience of finding Claude (in my own abstract way). Though planning an outcome in advance is not the typical approach with Intuitive Process Painting, the teachers gave me space and gently backed me up with the encouragement I needed to progressively get it all on paper.

I began each day with my morning walk, basking in the charms that embody the adobe-lined streets and peaceful, open desert spaces within walking distance from my cozy casita and the Mabel Luhan House. The healing power of the land was apparent, and I was mindful of soaking it all in, accessing morsels of peace and balance that I yearned for.

Given the circumstances, I wasn't feeling especially social. As you may know, grief tends to make us want to isolate and be alone. Grief aside, I'm not typically a group person, though there were plenty of opportunities to socialize with others in the living and dining areas during mealtime and on the lovely outside patio in between painting and classroom instruction. It felt somewhat reassuring to see some familiar faces of fellow classmates I had met the previous year.

One interaction stands out in my memory. The subject of Claude's suicide naturally came up in the conversation. The man I spoke to was in awe that I was still standing and able to be there as a workshop attendee, as opposed to crying my time away in bed. His response made me pause and wonder at the accomplishment of simply showing up to the workshop. This reinforced the sheer tenacity and courage it took for me to go, despite being in such a tenuous emotional state. It was especially difficult missing Micki's companionship. I felt lonely being there without her, but I did my best to stay focused on being gentle and loving with myself and my painting process. After all, that was one of the main reasons I was there.

With each passing day, it felt as if the soul of that mystical earth rose up, embracing me in its loving arms as I moved through the taxing five-day painting process. I felt incredibly proud of myself for having the audacity and determination to take that on, engage through the stream of tears, and find my way to resolution. Only I would know that embedded deep within all the shapes and colors was an image that held my beloved as I found him on that fateful day.

Looking back, I see that this experience may have been a metaphor for the journey through grief that lay ahead. In Intuitive Process Painting, we learn to trust that with each brushstroke and color choice, we will be guided to the next and so on, like steppingstones that let your intuition guide you as you trust in the simplicity and sanctity of the process itself.

But there was one difference: though the painting felt complete, my grief would live on. There is no endpoint, no finish line for one who grieves.

I had another desire that I hoped to fulfill while in Taos—to buy a new Turquoise ring. I had made the decision to remove my wedding band before the trip. It was a tough one, since I wasn't sure when it was appropriate to remove it, if ever. In the end, as with most other decisions I have made along the way, I waited until it simply felt *right*. Though I knew that I no longer wanted to wear it, I also sensed that having an unadorned ring finger would be a constant reminder that Claude was gone. The timing couldn't have been more perfect, Taos being the quintessential town to remedy this, as it has an abundance of handmade Native American turquoise jewelry to choose from. Turquoise has always been one of my favorite stones for its beauty and color variety. Some of its spiritual properties are those of protection, emotional healing and well-being, spiritual expansion, and creating a connection between heaven and earth.

I was on a quest, searching nearly every quaint shop on the historic Taos Plaza. After spending hours browsing and on the verge of giving up, I finally found not one but two rings that I liked. The added bonus came when the woman owner of the shop heard my story and spontaneously reached for a distinctive Native American basket overflowing with beautiful handmade scarves. She said, "please take one in honor of your proclamation of creating your new life." It was a noteworthy moment, and I felt particularly touched by her care and generosity. I thought that she may have been serving the purpose of sending a message from Claude or my angels, letting me know that I was on the right path, even now being loved and supported.

A sense of relief and empowerment washed over me—these rings were a symbol of my independence and a reminder that I could do this, that I *am* that powerful woman Claude always said I was. It felt good to have another task fulfilled, another steppingstone followed.

This trip was significant and entirely complementary with my intention. More layers and pieces of healing helped my new sense of self emerge as I re-built my heart. I felt eternally grateful that I had said YES to the adventure even in the face of all my fears trying their best to hold me back. I arrived home, embodying the gifts that were attained in the Land of Enchantment. These gifts boosted me to the next level, aligning me to the next stage of my grieving process.

*I allow my inner wisdom
& my divine feminine power
to guide me through this day.*

# IO

# TRUST

After a year of the dreaded firsts—my first birthday without Claude, our first wedding anniversary spent alone, the first Thanksgiving, Christmas, and New Year's, Claude's birthday, and Noah's birthday, to name a few—we were approaching springtime, which held the one that cut the deepest: the day of his suicide. If you have traveled at all in the world of grief, you know that anniversaries of any kind are tough. However, the first one can be the most difficult.

Noticing that the foreboding date was steadily gaining on me, Paige suggested that I attend a weekend grief camp offered by the Center for Good Grief where I saw her for our appointments. We both agreed that it might be another impactful opportunity to learn and be with others who had found themselves voyaging on the woeful ship called grief. Over the course of those two days, there were multiple methods through which we contacted and processed our grief. We participated in group counseling, group exercises that encouraged trust and bonding, art projects, and my personal favorite, taking part in ceremonial actions in which they demonstrated how to honor ourselves as grievers and recognize our lost loved ones.

One group activity that I found especially meaningful was the 'blindfold rope maze.' One by one, we were each led to the maze blindfolded. Our hands were placed on the rope and we were instructed to move around the maze until we found the end, which was the way out. It was announced repeatedly that if we needed assistance we could *ask for help*. I remember feeling determined that I could manage this on my own. But as time passed, I had not reached the end, even as I heard one after another participant being released, and I started to wonder where I had gone wrong. After merely a handful of us were left in the maze the facilitators asked us to remove our blindfolds. Much to my dismay, the rest of the people who had asked for help were all standing on the sidelines watching us grapple with how to find our way through.

In a short time, I learned that the purpose of this exercise was to attune to the lesson that it's ok to *ask for help*. I had to laugh at myself as I stood there feeling stunned and surprised. However, I recognized in an instant that even when we *feel* blindfolded and alone, floundering in our maze-like shadows of grief, help is always within reach and easily accessible if we are open to receiving.

Saving the best for last, they concluded the weekend with an awe-inspiring gathering called the balloon ceremony. The purpose of this ritual is to send blessings and love to our passed loved ones, adding another layer of letting go. We were each given our own yellow balloon, where we attached the name of our beloved and any message we felt called to convey to them. While each balloon was released into the vastness of the open sky, the names were spoken. It was a powerful, heart-opening ceremony that left us all in tears. It also served as a shining example of how something so simple can feel so sacred. Attending this workshop helped ignite the notion that we can find innumerable ways to celebrate those who are no longer in this life and the love that we still carry for them.

I'd had a reoccurring fantasy of going back to San Francisco to spread Claude's ashes in the spot where it all began for us, San

Francisco Bay. I had no idea how I could make that happen, but I knew that all things begin as an idea or a desire. After the balloon ceremony, I made the decision to set things in motion, and I put my trust in the Universe to lead the way to make my dream a reality.

In perfect synchronicity, my friend, Ann, who still lived in San Francisco knew someone who had a sailboat and was willing to take us out on the bay, therefore granting my wish. Divine timing was at play, as the availability of the boat perfectly coincided with Noah's spring break.

I prepared for the boat ceremony by gathering some things that I thought would be potent and meaningful inclusions. I began with some poems that held meaning for Claude while he was still alive and some memorable photos of the two of us in our prime, out on the boat with friends. I asked Marianne, who is a master at prayer creation, to write a prayer for Claude. Her spiritually-aware contribution fulfilled my desire to honor Claude's very existence in this life and beyond.

It was a sweet and intimate gathering, with just enough room on the boat to include the sailing crew, Noah, and a few close friends. The weather that day was picture perfect, and the bay was like glass. It was certainly better than a crazy, hold-on-to-your-hats rough and windy day, but there was not enough wind to actually fill the sails, so we had to motor all the way out and back. It was a bit disappointing missing out on the thrill of riding with the wind that I was so used to back in the day, but at the same time, I was grateful for the calm and peaceful waters, considering the whole point of the trip was to have a tranquil ceremony honoring Claude.

My mind wandered to a time long passed. I sat there dwelling in amazement that it had been thirteen years since I was out on San Francisco Bay with my dearest Claude. Feeling the surreal nature of this day, my heart ached as I remembered a simpler time. The familiar sights held dozens of joyful memories of the countless hours spent out there together. There had been no glimmer or foretelling of a future where I would be in this position of laying him to rest in the very spot where our love was ignited that first determining day on the boat.

When it came time to drop anchor and proceed with the ceremony, I felt my heart starting to race. My emotional response was predictable. I couldn't hold it together, and uncontrollable tears streamed down my face. Knowing this was likely to happen, I had already asked the others on board to carry out the readings of the prayer and poems.

Marianne wrote:

> *With grace and absolute knowing of the divine life expressing as ALL, we celebrate the life of the beloved expression known as Claude. Beyond all appearance, I know deeply that Claude's soul journey from the unseen to the seen and back into the unseen is blessed and a deep blessing—a blessing to all who knew him in the physical. A vibrant expression of grace, of humor, of laughter, of creativity, of strength and leadership, and especially one of kindness. His capacity to follow his dreams whole-heartedly and deeply, the blessing of the LOVE that he IS, the love that he still is, even beyond the physical expression of this beloved man, father, and husband. Claude is, absolutely, the LOVE that knows no bounds. We celebrate where he is now as the boundless, timeless LOVE ETERNAL. In this moment of his human experience, the love that emanated and embraced his beloved family, myself, and Noah, is felt deeply and will always be expressing continuously as he is the divine love that has never been born and can never die. It IS, HE IS, always ... and in all ways, the unconditional LOVE of the Divine itself.*
>
> *In such abiding reverent gratitude for the truth of Claude, we consecrate his earthly body today. We return it back from whence it came, from water back into water, from God back to God. With this ceremony, we sanctify the human expression of Claude,*

*allowing these waters to anoint his body temple and soul, to release any other earthly constraints, and to celebrate his freedom and his eternal being-ness. Divine perfection, having its way, beyond understanding, knowing that now, and forevermore, peace prevails. And so it is.*

The majority of Claude's ashes were wrapped in an elegant biodegradable vessel, although both Noah and I held on to a small portion to remember him by. After Noah relinquished the ashes into the water, we each had our turn casting purple rose petals in its wake—the same roses that had become 'our flower,' the same flowers that Claude arrived with as he was filled to the brim with anticipation at my doorstep back on the auspicious day of our first date. They had now morphed into a symbol of our beginning and our ending.

In order to create a sacred tone and a sense of reverence, I chose "Dante's Prayer" by Loreena McKennitt to fulfill my vision of a song accompaniment. As we ushered in the moment of releasing his material body, we invited his spirit to be released into the realm of divine love. We listened as she sang, "cast your eyes on the ocean," and we cast our eyes to the ocean. She went on, "Cast your soul to the sea," and we cast his ashes into the sea. "When the dark night seems endless, please remember me. Please remember me."

This song was the perfect accompaniment with its haunting lyrics and their poignant essence as we watched the petals slowly drift away on the gleaming, mirror-like surface of the water. My mission was now complete. I sensed that Claude was smiling and felt delighted that we had done that to honor his memory.

During the course of that first year, Gwen helped me consider his death from a new perspective. I began to see that rather than deeming his actions of 'committing' suicide as something horrific, I could view the decision to end this life as something that we all ultimately decide as divine beings. Though most of us are completely unconscious of this choice, at a soul level, we are in alignment with how we elect to leave.

Looking at it from this vantage point helped me put his actions into a broader understanding.

I chose to honor his decision with another ceremony on the first anniversary of his suicide, which was only one month after the boat ceremony. It caused me great sorrow and weighed heavily on my soul that I was not able to be with him when he took his final breath. In addition, it thoroughly tugged at my heart knowing that he left in such a grim manner, feeling utterly alone and downtrodden. Due to this, I wanted to create something meaningful to mark the day he made that fateful choice to end his life.

On the one year anniversary, while Noah was at school, I set up a chair in the doorway just outside the attic where he hung himself. At this point in time, I had worked through much of the fear around that room, but I would always feel some level of uneasiness being in and around it.

I set up a stone altar on the floor below where I found him hanging, just as I had done after his death. I burned sage and lit some white candles. I played "Dante's Prayer" again. Then, I simply sat in the chair and imagined bearing witness to him going through the motions of getting ready and ultimately reaching the point of no return when his spirit left his body. I was sobbing the whole time, wondering if I was crazy to be doing this, but it felt important. I couldn't think of any other way to make peace with the part of myself that desperately wished I could have been there to say goodbye as he was parting. In the end, it was healing for me to imagine going back in time, being fully and lovingly present, and supporting him as he made his transition. Though it was excruciatingly painful to go through, I was glad I followed my impulse. Once I was through the fire of those emotions, I felt soothed, and a sense of relief washed over me. I had healed another piece of my heart.

Grief is deeply personal. While Noah and I shared some ceremonies, we each needed our own process to say goodbye. While ordering the box to use for the boat ceremony, Noah had picked out a message in a bottle container for the portion of ashes that he kept. It seemed befitting with the nautical theme that was near and dear to Claude's heart. Having declared that he would live his life in the best possible manner to honor his father's memory, Noah inscribed a note to his dad that he rolled up and tucked into the bottle. To this day, I have no idea what he wrote; that will remain between father and son. Noah had not outwardly expressed a great deal of emotion or grief that first year, so this was a poignant moment showing me that he was recognizing his relationship with his dad in his own unique way.

As for my portion of ashes, I created a small altar space on a bookshelf. I included a cherished photo of us in a beaded frame of our favorite colors, blues and greens. In that timeless moment, we were in one another's arms, looking at the camera with beaming, light-filled smiles. It captured the true essence and simplicity of the time when our love was new and fresh. I added a candle, our wedding rings, and a few other things that felt appropriate to remember him by.

As you can imagine, each one of these occasions has required that I allow my emotions and my grief to be fully held. I have had to uncover an ever-deepening level of acceptance and surrender to what is. Through surrender comes peace; through surrender, we are shown 'the way.' Our natural tendency is to fight the current, which translates into resistance and struggle. If we allow the deluge of emotions to wash over us and maybe even engulf us for a time, we can find ourselves surrounded by peaceful waters, the calm after the storm. Grieving in this way, we are not hiding from our pain; we are not clutching and holding on for dear life. Rather, we are in the flow, feeling the full force of our feelings and honoring all that is.

You might ask: "How do I do this? I am too afraid that I will be swept away with the intensity of this pain." It's so incredibly challenging to maneuver through these tangled emotions that envelop us during these times. My answer is that we breathe, we breathe, and we breathe again. We say yes, we accept, we surrender, we feel it, we live it! When we can do this, we will find peace in the letting go. What shows up for us in these moments is needing our attention, and ultimately, needing our love. This will naturally take us to the next step, the next phase in this Widow's Moon. Without this surrender and allowing, we can get caught and ultimately trapped in a holding pattern that will lead to stagnation with our healing process.

With each and every breath, it takes immense bravery to dive into those troubled waters over and over again. It takes practice to develop *trust* in knowing we are always held in the loving arms of the Divine—*trust* that there is always a way through, *trust* that we will not drown in the depths never to be seen again.

*I trust that*
*I am always held*
*in the loving arms*
*of the Divine.*

# II

# INTUITION

Trusting our inner guidance system or intuition, we can experience miracles beyond our wildest dreams. The more we practice, the more we are able to trust. In turn, the more we trust, the easier it becomes to align with our soul's purpose. I have observed this repeatedly through all my life's passages and the miraculous results that arise time and time again.

As Thanksgiving arrived, we were getting used to filling in the void that Claude left with our own life's musings, but grief was still welling up in my heart, especially during Noah's holiday break.

For the second year in a row, Claude wasn't there to ceremoniously cut the turkey. Truth be told, though, Noah didn't even like turkey, so chicken became the new norm for us—but I still made the cranberry sauce and stuffing just to make it feel like a somewhat 'normal' Thanksgiving.

Our house was feeling safe again, and up until this point, I had resigned myself to the fact that we would stay put until Noah graduated from high school two years down the road. I had no intention of taking him away from his best friend and the school he seemed to be doing so well in. Just as importantly, I thought I was in no condition to make a major move.

Much to my astonishment, the day after Thanksgiving, Noah sat me down to reveal a notion that would dramatically alter the orientation of our lives. In much the same manner as when he announced that he would parent himself, he proclaimed that he felt it was time to relocate. He said he was starting to outgrow the place where he had spent his childhood and that he didn't see a future for himself there.

I could see that this was a potent developmental moment for him as a fifteen-year-old. Though I was in shock that he had reached this momentous decision on his own, I was also in awe as I witnessed one of his first major life decisions based on his own inner guidance system. It was a strange sensation to acknowledge that he knew it was our time to leave before I did. Fortunately for Noah, I had lived this way for my entire adult life, so I understood where he was coming from. Each time I made a move to a new location, I heard the call to leave—usually several months or years in advance. I always knew it was time to move on by listening and learning to trust my intuition over time. Because of this, I knew the signs. Noah was clearly being guided and was tuned into a higher plan that we needed to act on ASAP if we were to make this work to our benefit.

I admit that I did have some hesitation since I am not known to be good with sudden changes, especially since I was just feeling settled and accepting that we would be there for a few more years. It's funny—Claude would have been proud of the way Noah sold the idea to me since that was one of Claude's superpowers. He had clearly given this a lot of thought, and with his persuasive rationalizations, it only took a few minutes of discussion for me to get on board. We decided we would wait until he finished out his school year the following spring, but in the meantime, there was an inordinate amount of planning to do. The potentiality of this far-reaching commitment left me buzzing with a barrage of emotions: excitement, anticipation, dread, and fear.

All in all, though, it felt like favorable timing and a highly desirable direction to move towards.

I never felt a strong attachment to Memphis even after fifteen years of living there. Then, the connection was further frayed by Claude's suicide. Now, moving was a compelling opportunity to start over. But even with our eagerness to move, the daunting task of getting our home ready to put on the market, packing, and buying a new home felt overwhelming to me, to say the least. I wondered how I would have the endurance to get through that. I knew I would have to reach out for a great deal of assistance to help us make this ambitious and purposeful transition.

Once the decision was made, Noah and I had several conversations about what we were each looking for with this move. It felt important that this be a joint endeavor. After all, Noah was the impetus for this pivotal opportunity to co-create a new life. We were on the cusp of manifesting a lifestyle that would enhance and support us in ways that were not currently available. We generated specific guidelines and qualities we were seeking in our new home. As we narrowed down our options, we weighed the pros and cons of various locations. In the end, we decided on Boulder, Colorado. Culturally, it felt more in line with my beliefs. It had all of the natural beauty I needed, along with good schools and close proximity to both my sister and my dear friend Aztechan, who lived in Denver with her own family. Beyond that, Gwen would be visiting to see her daughter in Colorado Springs, and Stacey, my trusted financial advisor, claimed Colorado was her "happy place." She and her family had been making yearly visits, so I would see her as well. In short, it fit the bill on so many levels that we decided to go for it.

I had come to rely on my financial advisors for all my major life choices since Claude died. First and foremost on my agenda was to organize a meeting with my team to discuss our plan. I was nervous and felt uncertain about how they would respond. Would they think I was crazy? Would they think it was an unwise financial or personal move? I had no idea what their reaction might be.

Much to my relief, they were all 100% on board with an outpouring of enthusiasm and support. After I revealed why I had asked them all to convene on my behalf, it almost felt like they wanted to stand up and cheer. They had seen me through the darkest hour of my life, and I felt their genuine desire for both Noah and me to find peace and happiness. After explaining our reasons for choosing Boulder, they genuinely understood and thought it made perfect sense, given what they knew about us and what our interests were.

At this meeting, I also revealed that when I moved to Boulder, I would start using my middle name, Hope. Where did that inspiration come from? As it so happened, the good old kitchen sink transmission center came through for me once again while I was doing the dishes. I had never liked my given name, Carolyn. Suddenly, I clearly heard that going by my middle name would be significant in the creation of my new calling in life. I even heard Cara in the mix, but Hope rang the loudest. I had no idea at that moment what my new life purpose might look like, but I took this guidance to heart, and with the move, the timing seemed synchronistic. Even so, I felt a little nervous. I had considered changing my name in the past but never had the courage to do so. This may have been the Universe's way of kicking me in the butt and saying, "it's time!" I was sincerely touched as they all loved that idea and started calling me Hope right away. What more could I have asked for? I was overwhelmed with a sense of gratitude and felt a huge sense of relief to have their full, unfettered support with this next major, life-altering direction.

One day, in the midst of our planning, Noah and I were standing in the kitchen. Seemingly out of the blue, Noah said plainly to me, "Mom, you know we have to sell our house in Asheville. It's time; it's old energy that needs to be released." I just stood there looking at him for a couple of seconds. I wondered how he had developed such an acute level of understanding and awareness. Then the most obvious answer flooded my consciousness. Why hadn't I thought of this before? The two years of working with Gwen opening his perceptions and connection to Source had led us to this instant. I knew that as painful as it would be to sell, he was right on the money. In fact, I had thought about it myself in passing, but with everything happening so quickly, I just hadn't gotten to the particulars yet.

Not too long after that talk with Noah, I had a phone conversation with Stacey. She echoed the same thing that he told me. She said, "You know you will have to sell the Asheville house." I sighed and said, "I know." She was surprised with the ease with which I was surrendering to this realization. I told her that Noah had beaten her to the punch. I had already come to realize that it was an important step for me to relinquish my dream home, just like every other part of our previous reality. But despite knowing it was necessary and the best thing for us in the long run, it still saddened me deeply to have to let go of something else that had meant so much to me.

With all of that in place, I was eager and ready to make the move come together as smoothly as possible. I was a woman on a mission. I am the type of person who dives headfirst into challenges and gives all I have to make something happen. This doesn't mean that I won't have any fear or question myself. It just means that when it feels intuitively on the mark, I will become obsessed until I have achieved my goal, riding those waves of fear until I reach the shore arriving at my desired target.

I received advice from Stacey about a prudent price range for our new home and a plan for how to buy it. It was starting to come together. Now, it was up to me to find a realtor in Boulder. I did an online search and came across a man that looked like someone I would like to work with. I saw Zachary's videos on his website and felt intuitively that he was the one who would help us buy our new home. As it turned out, he was amazing. He went above and beyond for us and has remained a trusted friend.

Thankfully, this was not my first home-buying experience. Otherwise, doing this on my own without Claude would have felt much more intimidating. Instead, I knew what to expect and how to search for potential homes online. I looked at properties daily, but at first, nothing was grabbing my attention. Unfortunately, the winter wasn't the most opportune time to be looking at real estate. After about a month, I started feeling discouraged and a bit worried. Despite this, I continued with my research on the various areas within the city to get clear on where I wanted to live. Once I reached more clarity and honed in on my preferred neighborhood and home type, a promising listing came on the market within three days.

This was a perfect example of the Laws of Attraction in action. I had seen this in my life and those of others around me multiple times. It is truly astounding—once we are clear on what we want or feel we need, the Universe generally falls in line. It's important to let go of the perceived or precise way to reach our desired result and trust that the outcome is exactly what is required for our highest good. Learning to trust in the way it is delivered can be challenging. I am sometimes dismayed when things don't appear to be moving quickly enough. But I have learned that all will unfold in divine timing.

As I opened the link for the property listing that appeared on that third day, my heart started pounding with the very first photo, then the second, then the third, and soon I could hardly contain my enthusiasm. I felt with great certainty that this was *the one*; I felt it with my whole body. I immediately called Zach. We discussed it, and he agreed to go see the townhouse first thing the next morning. He did a thorough walkthrough and took some extra photos of things that were not shown in the online listing. With each new photo that he sent to me I was getting even more excited. Overall, he said it looked like a good solid property with no major issues.

Since I was not physically in Boulder to see it myself, he asked me if I wanted to put in an offer sight unseen. Due to the highly competitive real estate market, we both knew that if I didn't jump on it right away, someone else would. Without hesitation, I said yes. We worked out a price, and he presented our offer by noon that same day. After anxiously waiting all afternoon for a response from the seller,

I got a call later in the evening from Zach saying, "Congratulations, they've accepted your offer, and you are officially under contract!" I was thrilled; this dream was quickly becoming a reality!

Many around me were mystified that I would have the audacity to sign a contract without ever setting foot inside. Oddly enough, this only fueled my fire. Yes, I agree this was a bold move for sure, something Claude would have done. I learned well from him. But what they didn't understand was that I was also accessing my own seasoned abilities to fully trust my intuition, and I felt with my whole being that this was our new home. It was a given that I had to follow through and take the necessary steps and some calculated risks to make it happen. To this day, Zach tells that story of one of his clients who took the bull by the horns and just dove in head-first.

In another stroke of divine timing, I had already purchased our plane tickets for the following week to visit Colorado. We had planned to meet with Zach in person, look at some other listings, and get more familiar with Boulder. But thankfully, looking at other properties was unnecessary now. Noah and I arrived at the townhouse filled with nervous anticipation on a cool, sunny January day, not quite two months after we made that radical choice to move. We could hardly believe this was all happening as we waited for Zach to join us on the front patio of our future home. After our introductions, we eagerly went inside for the grand tour. It was all that I had imagined and then some. It was hard to fully grasp from the photos online just how stunning the location is. This part of Boulder is imbued with the magnificent mountain scenery just steps outside the door, with walking and hiking trails in abundance. I was enthralled with the beauty that surrounded our new home. Within days, it was a relief to have the inspection behind us. Then, it was full speed ahead onto the closing inside of three weeks. Gratitude filled my heart, acknowledging that Claude left us well taken care of. I could now imagine the two of us embarking on this new adventure even more concretely.

We all have this ability to follow our higher guidance; it simply requires a commitment, practice, and a willingness to allow our inner voice or our inner wisdom to play a central part in our lives. It may not feel comfortable at first to peek out from the refuge of your grief. You can start by being aware of that small whisper or subtle tap on the shoulder that you may typically ignore. Or maybe it's a loud voice. In either case, you can start at this moment if you desire. Once you make the commitment, you are on your way to accessing the light of your soul. It really is quite simple; you just need to listen and then act on your inner nudging and watch as things unfold, as if by magic. Over time, you will develop more confidence as you see the outcomes you have been guided to reach. You have the wisdom of the ages residing within you. You and only you have all of the answers at your fingertips. Will you join me on this quest for the truth that dwells with you as YOU?

*I trust that my intuition*
*is guiding me*
*to co-create*
*the life that is*
*for my highest good.*

# 12

# GATEWAY

Having closed on the townhome in late January, I was now officially a proud new homeowner in Colorado. At the time, Boulder had been voted the #1 happiest city for several years. Knowing we could use a good dose of that, I figured we were heading to the right place. We were on the cusp of a new reality that felt liberating and expansive, and we both looked forward to embarking on a new adventure and new chapter in our lives. Receiving help from our angels, or Claude, or both seemed to have become the norm while things fell easily into place as if sparkly pixie dust had been scattered throughout the entire process.

Once on track with our new home, it was time to wrap things up with our old one. The enormous undertaking of getting the house ready to put on the market was my next big hurdle. I put together pages of checklists with all of the things that needed repairs, painting, or other attention and then hired a handyman who slowly whittled away at these items. It seemed like an endless task, but day by day and week by week, we soon accomplished our goal.

My next project was to find a realtor who I felt comfortable working with to list our house. Stacey came through once again by referring me to her realtor, Molly, who turned out to be another of the many angels we had helping us along this journey. She was, in one word, amazing! The acquired possessions that filled our home held the remnants and memories of our life as a complete, intact family. Sorting through these items was a profoundly emotional process. Sometimes, it felt as if I were drowning in a sea of sludge, soon to be swallowed up by my feelings. Molly compassionately held my hand through the completion stage. She exceeded expectations by beautifully staging the house, making it look like something that you might see in a magazine. She hired her professional photographer, which added the final touch. Within a few days, we were ready to go live.

After months of preparation and relentless hard work, we set a date for the open house in March. Thankfully, all our time and energy paid off, with record numbers at the open house and three offers after only three days on the market. The buyers even agreed to a longer-than-usual closing date since we needed to wait for Noah to finish school. Once again, it had all fallen into place relatively easily—another validation that we were indeed on the right path.

The move was a major distraction. Now, with about two months left to go, there were even more lists to create and plow through. For the most part, my grief was on the back burner. It was an intensely stressful time, but it also served as a respite. My total focus had to be on making this move go as smoothly as possible.

Looking back, I'm not sure how I was able to keep it all together and stay so organized. My neighbor reinforced this by expressing that I was exceptionally good at getting things done. I had known that about myself, but coordinating this move, finding and buying another home, and keeping track of all the other details involved with this leap of faith was a massive undertaking under any circumstances. To have successfully accomplished all of this was impressive and empowering for me. I had come to rely on Claude over the years for certain things. We would typically divide and conquer when faced with challenges.

This time, I was on my own. Though Claude was not physically present, I have no doubt that he was working behind the scenes to help me as he could from the other side. It was a formidable task, but I made it through with flying colors, which felt like a huge victory.

Gwen had become one of our trusted friends over those two years we had worked with her. She repeatedly urged me to take the time for one last visit to our Asheville house before our move. She even offered to drive me the eight hours or so that it took to get there by car, as she knew that long distance driving was stressful for me. I was under a tremendous amount of pressure, so I was hesitant to add one more thing into the mix. The thought of selling the dream mountain home that I loved and had hoped to live in one day weighed heavily on my heart. Despite my hesitation, and after giving it much thought, I agreed it would be in my best interest to go for one final visit. I recognized that I needed to take that time to make peace and say goodbye, formally closing that chapter of our lives.

On the drive, I felt more apprehensive with each hour that passed. The days of happy anticipation that I typically felt as we got closer were behind me, never to be experienced again. There was the additional trigger that my whole life had changed and that Claude was gone. Yet, at the same time, I held the excitement and joy in my heart of starting a new life in Colorado. This was simply one of the many required rungs on the ladder that I needed to climb in order to relinquish our past, putting it in its proper place.

The plan was to spend a few days going through our belongings to see if there was anything I wanted to hold onto and bring to Colorado. We also intended to perform some clearing and releasing ceremonies so that the property would be unimpeded energetically, with the hope of expediting an offer to purchase. At that point, it had already been on the market for a few months with no major interest. Since I held such an emotional attachment to this property, we sensed these ceremonies would help free things up for another potential owner to step in with no residual resistance on my part.

It also felt particularly important to take some time to breathe it all in and press the pause button from the hubbub of the previous months. I yearned for this respite that our dear Sunset Haven could provide. I craved the quiet, and I needed the time to reflect and process all that had happened. Over the course of six years, those mountains and trees had become my friends, and the home had been my sacred sanctuary.

It was a dream of mine years ago when Claude and I first met to have a retreat center. This home was the closest I came to realizing that dream. I had created a beautiful healing space for others to come to visit, finding peace and solitude. Since we had used the home as a vacation rental, we had a guest book full of touching stories from visitors expressing their heartfelt gratitude. There were marriage proposals, family reunions, girls' weekend gatherings, romantic getaways—you name it. Some of the stories brought tears to my eyes. I felt saddened at the thought of not being a part of that anymore.

Those three days were a mix of tears, laughter, joy, and sorrow. On the morning of our departure, I stood on the wrap-around deck overlooking the magnificent view, teary-eyed. I thanked the trees, the mountains, the birds, and the land for all they had given me during my stay with them over those years we were so fortunate to be there. Because I had listened to Gwen's urgings with her timeless wisdom, I felt more calm and grateful. She was correct: that one last visit would be an important springboard, launching me onto the next phase of letting go. On the final night, we watched the sun set for the last time over the horizon of that wonderful sea of green.

I landed back home and back to the reality of finishing up for the big moving day, which was only three weeks away. Those weeks were jam-packed full of saying goodbye to friends, Noah finishing up with his school, and on and on.

Then, moving day was upon us with a mad barrage of activity. I was spread so thin and stressed beyond belief, yet I was ecstatic that this day had finally arrived. After six months of preparation, it would soon be over. Some last-minute packing still had to be done on the morning the moving truck arrived. But thanks to Claude's mom, Eleanor (who was our expert packer) along with some neighbors' help, we completed it all by the skin of our teeth.

The movers barely fit all our things on the truck. In fact, we had to leave some lawn furniture that didn't make it in. I was disappointed, but at that point, I honestly didn't care anymore. With the truck expertly packed, it was filled to capacity, floor to ceiling and front to back. We all stood there holding our breath, hoping they would be able to close the doors and lock it up for the long drive to Colorado. Fortunately, they were successful, and we all breathed a collective sigh of relief. They drove off with all our worldly belongings, and one by one, the neighbors left. The endless hours of frenzy gave way to a silent and still house, nearly barren of any sign of our stay for the last fifteen years. Begrudgingly, Noah and I still had one more task in front of us—a quick clean-up of the house. I was desperately exhausted at this point in the late afternoon, but somehow, I found the strength and was able to plow through it. Then, we were done. The sense of relief I felt was immense. I could hardly move.

I had a ritual that I started years ago when it was time to move from my home. Just as I had done in the Asheville house, I would pause and take a few closing minutes to look around the space and give thanks. Feeling mixed emotions, the memories of the past always flashed through my mind. This time was no exception.

We went into the living room of this now empty, lifeless house that was once our home. We sat on the stoop of the fireplace that Claude had so carefully and beautifully tiled years before in one of our many remodeling projects. It was a bittersweet moment. I was flooded with tender sensations—tears of joy, of nostalgia, and of pain. Noah had grown up there, and we spent most of our marriage in that house. Many of those memories brought me great joy. Watching our son grow up seemed like the most notable at that time. But that defining moment of Claude's death taking place there was the one thing that I was the most grateful to be leaving behind. I was completely unaware at the time that there was really no escaping the impact or the memories of that moment when I found him. I could leave the house behind, but the trauma and the images would follow and haunt me for years to come.

Saying our goodbyes to Claude's mom and sister was something that I was not looking forward to. I had no idea in that moment of our last embrace if I would ever have the courage to return. But in my heart, I knew I didn't want to.

That goodbye was our last stop before heading to Betty's to spend our last night in Tennessee. Gwen was waiting there since she had offered to drive us to Colorado. After Claude died, Betty's house had become an oasis for Noah and me. That was where we would meet with Gwen for our monthly healing sessions, eventually seeing Betty as well for her transformative and soothing bodywork sessions. The two of them, in combination, kept us afloat and contributed greatly to our healing process during those first two years. It seemed fitting, then, that we would spend our last night there with Gwen and Betty before setting out to Boulder the next morning with Gwen in the driver's seat. When we arrived, we were welcomed with a calming meal and soothing environment, cushioning our frenetic day.

I woke up in her house the next morning feeling sleep-deprived, disoriented, exhausted, and thankful that there remained only one more important yet crucial step for me to complete before bidding my final farewell to Memphis. Yet, the final task that lay before me was to sign the papers to close on my house. I drove to Molly's office, feeling sleepy and a bit numb. It felt oddly unsettling yet exciting all at once—another moment of realization that my whole world was changing. This was really happening.

I was leaving the past fifteen years of my life behind me. I was leaving the place where my husband ended his life. It felt like I was on the precipice of something *big*, as if I were standing at the edge of the Grand Canyon with all of its expanse and majesty. I had done it! I had created this gateway to my new life and, in many ways, a new identity, even down to my intention to go by a new name.

Mercifully, the closing on the house went through without a hitch. Molly presented me with a farewell gift and a tearful hug. We had developed a great deal of affection for one another through it all, and she made the entire experience much more bearable. We said our goodbyes and expressed gratitude for our time together. I headed back to Betty's for our final send-off. Then away we drove, heading west filled with expectancy and eagerness as we rolled state by state into new and undiscovered territory.

*I give myself permission
to live,
to laugh,
to feel joy
& peace again.*

# 13

# HOPE

We arrived in Boulder three days later, overtired but buzzing and eager to begin this new chapter. After half a year of preparation, the highly anticipated day had finally arrived. Colorado distinguishes itself by having 300-plus days of sunshine per year. This particular morning in late May was among those and did not disappoint. The weather was ideal for our movers to unpack all our worldly possessions. The process of finding a trustworthy moving company and receiving everything in one piece is always nerve-wracking. Once again, we were watched over, and all went according to plan.

It seemed that we had just stepped inside when we were promptly greeted at the front door by one of our new neighbors, who was bubbling with enthusiasm to welcome us to the neighborhood. I was now presented with the opportunity to try out using my 'new' name, Hope. It felt a bit awkward, and I found myself needlessly explaining that it was actually my middle name but that I wanted to start fresh in a new town as Hope. As we continued talking, I discovered that one of her daughters' names was Cara. If that wasn't enough, she told me that there was another woman named Hope living across from me. If you remember, when I was invited by my inner guidance to start using Hope as my first name, I also heard Cara. What are the chances that *both* names would be represented in such close proximity? Was this another sign that we were indeed on the right path? It sure felt that way.

Once the young men were finished unloading the truck and we exchanged our best wishes, we were left with another monumental task of unpacking and organizing our new home. I normally enjoy this part as it's somewhat of a creative undertaking to construct a new living environment. But this time I was so physically worn out that I just stood there staring, frozen in place. We had downsized from a 3,000-square-foot suburban house to a 1,500-square-foot townhome. I had given away or sold a good majority of our belongings, but we still had an inordinate number of things that needed to be organized and arranged. There were boxes stacked up literally everywhere in our smaller quarters, and it felt suffocating. To my amazement, I quickly discovered another one of Gwen's many gifts—her mastery at organizing a compact space. In my dazed and confused state of mind, she seriously saved the day with this supercharged ability! Before we knew it, things were starting to take shape.

Waking up the next morning in my cozy new bedroom, the warm light shining in around the dark edges of the blackout curtains, I felt the weight and the breadth of my old reality securely behind me. I lay there in bed, still weary after a long sleep, wondering how I would have the endurance to 'make things happen' yet again. It felt like I had stretched myself to the limits by getting us this far. Had I hit the proverbial wall? Truthfully, I am not sure what I would have done without Gwen, this remarkable woman who had seen me through two of the most formidable years of my life while holding space for Noah and me through all our trials in addition to our joys. She was there for me now, loving me unconditionally, seeing me at my worst yet still showing up and helping me stay calm. Taking one step at a time, we gradually chipped away at the boxes that had overtaken our townhome. Before long, we had created a new backdrop for our ever-evolving lives that would be revamped over time. For now, though, it felt tamed, and a sense of relief was starting to wash over me.

The time swiftly approached for Gwen to pass the torch back to me. I had been leaning on her over that previous week, but after a few short days in Boulder, I was starting to feel more grounded. It was time for me to fly solo again. I was immensely grateful for all that she had contributed to our well-being. Again, we were being watched over and cared for with another angelic intervention in Gwen. Because of our close friendship, parting was painful—yet another letting go. But on the upside, her daughter lived in Colorado Springs, so we would certainly be seeing her again in Colorado. Knowing this helped soothe our hearts and soften our tearful farewell.

After Gwen's departure, it was just the two of us in this semi-unfamiliar world. For the first time in months, I was not on a tight schedule to accomplish something every minute of the day. Sure, I still had an assortment of affairs to take care of, but the pace could be at my choosing. I was no longer held captive by time; I could simply and slowly breathe it all in.

Noah and I unanimously agreed that we wanted to press pause on our to-do list and connect with my dear friend, Aztechan, her three daughters, and her husband, who lived close by in Denver. We had already seen them twice that year when we stayed with them during our trips to Colorado. After purchasing the home, we'd been back in March during Noah's spring break to meet the high school officials, shop for new furniture, and set up some home improvement projects to be completed before we moved in.

It was hard to believe that Aztechan and I finally lived within a mere 40-minute drive after so many years of living great distances from one another. We'd sensed our 'soul sister' connection from the moment we met in California two years before Noah was born. She was a fellow massage therapist who shared her friendship as well as her knowledge of aromatherapy with me. Our lives went in different directions when

Claude, Noah, and I moved from Pacifica to Memphis, but because of our cherished and loving friendship, we had stayed in touch as our lives unfolded over those years. Now we would be able to see each other often, with our kids having the opportunity to develop their own relationships. Given that Noah is an only child, I hoped this might potentially fill that gap for him. As luck would have it, Noah and Aztechan's youngest daughter, Bianca, had the opportunity to develop a strong, sibling-like connection that persists to this day.

The business of settling into a new city and a new home can be exciting and daunting all at the same time. This was no exception. Fortunately, we had the summer to acclimate without Noah being in school. He took full advantage of his free time and went into high gear, tapping into the same entrepreneurial spirit that his dad had embodied. He created flyers and advertised on the neighborhood Nextdoor website. He targeted our surrounding area to advertise babysitting, pet sitting, and dog walking services. Before long, he had several clients in all three categories, and the cash was flowing in. He felt empowered to create a profitable and satisfying niche for himself. I couldn't help but feel proud of his accomplishments and impressed by his ability to generate and manifest his desired outcomes. It seemed apparent that Claude was by his side, cheering him on and helping him make this happen.

As if divinely appointed, Paul Selig just happened to have an in-person workshop in Boulder in late June just a few weeks after we got there. I was beyond excited to have this opportunity to be in person with Paul and the Guides. Noah was still exploring the spiritual and metaphysical world, so he was interested in attending with me. Noah was by far the youngest attendee. Since Paul had previously been a college professor for many years, he seemed to embrace Noah's presence and enjoy his curious mind. The other attendees were all in awe of this young one who was already on 'the path' of self-exploration and spiritual growth at just sixteen years of age, perhaps imagining how different their lives would have been if they had started sooner.

We were invited to ask questions of the Guides and Paul at various times throughout the workshop. As one might expect, only two years out from Claude's suicide, I was still interested in receiving further insights or guidance around this. The main messages that stuck with me were that he was sorry beyond words for all the pain he had caused and that he wasn't in his right mind at the time. He stressed that *it was not my fault* and that we would see each other again. Tears welled up as I heard these words once more. I was grateful to know that since I had heard this from several sources up to this point, it must actually be true.

Overall, the workshop was quite satisfying, and I made some new meaningful connections. A fellow workshop attendee named Lisa, who lived in Boulder, announced that she was starting a Paul Selig book study group, which helped me over the initial social hump. It was nice to have some like-minded women to spend time with on a regular basis. The group would eventually run its course, but Lisa became a walking buddy. Her friendship, love, and support would help sustain me for the next few years until her eventual move.

Months before moving to Boulder, I had also discovered Matt Licata's writings by way of a woman I met in Asheville in one of Marianne's groups. I was mesmerized by his eloquent musings about radically loving and caring for all aspects of ourselves right where we are at any given moment. He encourages us to celebrate and deeply honor it all: the part that grieves, the part that resides in anger or fear, the part that feels shame, and joy, and so on. Matt lives in Boulder and was doing a weekend workshop with Jeff Foster, who is equally engaging and whose teachings are much the same as Matt's. As with Paul's workshop, Noah decided to join me. It was an amazing experience, and once again, the other workshop attendees were in awe of Noah as he stood up, asking his pointed questions. Matt and Jeff's teachings felt reassuring and nurturing like a soothing, healing balm for my still-grieving heart. This was indeed another auspicious welcoming to our new city both within the first two months of our arrival.

Meanwhile, the Asheville house lingered on the market, with no interest in six months. So, it was a huge relief when the tables turned by mid-July when we suddenly found ourselves with multiple offers. It was a unique property, so it needed just the right family to buy it. I was happy to know that the buyers would continue using it as a vacation rental for a few years before they moved in themselves, and that our regular guests would still be able to enjoy it. With that emotionally weighted endeavor behind me, I could close yet another episode in this saga. At that point, so much had transpired that my feelings about selling it had shifted from heartbreak to relief. It was one less thing from my past that I needed to contend with.

Time was flying by. Before we knew it, August had arrived, and school was in session. One of the many things to appreciate about our new location was that it was a short walk to Noah's high school. It was actually one of the things I put on my wish list when I was envisioning our new home. He was free to come and go as he pleased, as they have an open campus. I was released from my daily duty of driving him to and from school, and he received the opportunity to create more autonomy in his life. It felt liberating for us both. Although Noah had his driver's license, he was still not ready for driving on his own. So, for now, it was his bicycle, walking, or the bus that would get him to where he needed to go. Fortunately, Boulder is a very bike-and bus-friendly city, so this worked out well for him.

Starting in a new school at any age is tough, and in high school even more so. Despite that, Noah took on the challenge. After all, it was his idea to start fresh in a new town. On my recommendation, he connected with the woman in charge of the gifted program and found a friend and ally in her. He was fortunate to make two close friends fairly quickly, which had historically been a place of challenge for him. He has always been different, not your 'typical' child. He has been, in many ways, miles ahead of the majority of his peers. He is highly gifted in several areas, sometimes making it hard to relate to others.

But with age and lots of inner work, he was maturing and surely on his way to becoming an amazing young man.

By the end of the summer, I was ready for a change too. I decided to trade in my loyal Toyota van that had served us well. I had taken a lot of teasing for the fact that I drove a van, but I didn't care—it was perfect for me. With all seats down, I could easily fit all my canvasses in the back. It also came in handy each summer traveling to "Sunset Haven." It never failed me when I needed to fill it to the brim with art supplies, Noah's summer camp supplies, and various other things we needed to bring with us. It wasn't that I didn't like it anymore or that it was an old van; it was actually in perfect condition. But it was a piece of my story and part of the purge that needed to happen to release more of that old energy. I traded it in for the quintessential Colorado automobile, a Subaru. It was in the budget that Stacey laid out for me, and it fulfilled all my needs.

In this undertaking, I was surely missing Claude's level of expertise in buying cars. Over the years, I had watched him purchase several new vehicles. I think on some level he enjoyed the cat-and-mouse car-buying game. He was in sales himself, so he knew all the moves. But he wasn't here, and I was once again faced with something that felt pretty intimidating. So, I did my research and was able to actually work with a woman at the dealership who helped me home in on the car that was right for me. I may not have gotten the deal that Claude would have, but I think I did better than okay. Most importantly, I got through it. This was another milestone for me, and I felt proud of myself for this significant accomplishment. When I got my new driver's license and auto registration, it was official; I was now a bona fide resident of Colorado with my brand-new trusty Subaru Forester as my steady sidekick.

*I allow the light of my soul
to shine brightly, illuminating
my path through grief*

# 14

# ADAPTATION

The breezy days of autumn had emerged with yellow leaves glowing against the cool blue Colorado skies. Keeping in pace with the turn of the season, I fell into a period of contemplation. I looked back in awe at the sheer number of alterations that had been woven into the many-hued fabric of my life over the past two years. Though I may have gone through those years at times literally kicking and screaming, I marveled at my ability to adapt to change, yielding to its transformative essence.

By this time, I'd developed a daily rhythm of interaction with my newly discovered surroundings. I noticed that the trees, with all their wisdom, are our teachers. They exemplify the ability to gently and effortlessly release that which no longer serves us. I also noticed that nature does not resist the cycles of change. Let's think for a moment. Do the leaves on the trees resist letting go? Do the flowers resist blooming? Do the grasses resist turning brown and moving freely with the blustering wind? In fact, the only thing nature *does* resist is stagnation or lack of change.

All things are in flux. Yet as humans, our inclination is to cling to the known each time we are presented with ever-foreboding *change*.

But just as in the natural world, change over time contains the bounty of rebirth. If we could only recognize that we, too, are part of this inherent order, we would have more space to breathe and appreciate this wild mystery ride.

Though I had been progressing wholeheartedly on the wave of change to the best of my ability, the massive number of adjustments I had undergone had taken their toll on my physical body. My health had declined from all that I had been dealing with since Claude's death. Between grief, trauma, moving, and major adaptations on all fronts, the stress of it all had an impact. I was at a tipping point, and my body said *enough*!

Taking a cue from the trees around me, I chose to embrace a season of quietude and, in a sense, reverse course. After so much forward movement, it was finally time to slow down and tend to my physical, emotional, and spiritual well-being. With the all-consuming attention to detail that the move required, I had gotten off track from that process. I wanted to go deeper and learn what was required to support my healing at this stage of my journey. This intuitively felt like the single most important thing I could do for myself moving forward.

As always, I was out and active every morning, yet it was becoming evident that I didn't have the physical stamina and strength to take full advantage of all the picturesque hiking trails in Boulder. Since this was part of the allure of our move, I was disappointed. But, as I often noticed, the situation was actually in ideal alignment to my needs. We lived within walking distance from a lake within the bounds of one of the most gorgeous parks in Boulder. The lake served to quench my desire for water in Boulder's dry climate, and the walking paths were well-suited to my abilities and energy levels. The most extraordinary feature of the park was that it possessed one of the finest mountain views in the city. In short, it was the needed remedy during this time of healing and soon became one of my coveted sanctuaries.

Even so, my reserves were running on empty as I struggled to keep up with my daily responsibilities. Once again, I began the process of finding the support I needed to heal in this new city.

Both Noah and I continued our work with Gwen's powerful energy healing sessions by phone and in person when we were lucky enough to have her visit Colorado. Marianne was still in the mix, adding her remote healing sessions and some potent online courses. Yet I also wanted in-person support.

It was encouraging to come across the Grief Support Network (GSN) here in Boulder. Their philosophy was in sync with mine around processing grief and the role it plays in our lives, and I couldn't have been more pleased. In addition, their practitioner network proved to be a veritable gold mine. It included an array of accomplished practitioners trained in various modalities to support those who were grieving. I couldn't wait to dive into such a vast ocean of potential.

Knowing how much I value massage, it's not surprising that I got the show on the road with a massage therapist, Eeris, who I discovered in the GSN listings. Her intuitive angelic presence and her energy work were exactly what I needed and gave me the first piece of my revitalized transmutation puzzle. Next, I found Mark, a chiropractor who uses a non-force chiropractic method. Thanks to his ever-present empathetic nature and his personal experience of grief, I immediately felt supported and understood. Mark and Eeris have both been there every step of the way as I have moved through this very long season of grief. To this day, their work has served to assist my body energetically and physically, helping to bring balance to my nervous system. Thanks to my reassembled healing team, I was soon back on the road to restoration.

Getting support with the grief was, oddly enough, the easiest piece. It was even more challenging to address my trauma after the hellish experience of finding Claude. Yet this part of me needed all the more attention. Recognizing this as a gradual process, I had been chipping away at the effects of that fateful moment in time before I got to Boulder. But I knew I needed more help sifting through the layers of the rubble left in my troubled memory banks.

Attending to this issue seemed to be the key to unlocking this experience in my psyche. I wanted to work with someone who specialized in EMDR therapy, which is used to help process traumatic memories. I had experienced this therapy in the past. By revisiting a memory or belief while focusing on external stimuli, we can seek to transform our associations and perspectives. I chose Linda, another GSN list provider. Surprisingly, she had actually met my sister at a Vision Quest training workshop years ago. I was impressed with her ability to expertly assist me as I processed this traumatic event. With her stellar abilities, she guided me through some of the most emotionally painful terrain imaginable. After several months of working with her, I felt I had gone as far as I could go, and honestly, I needed a break. I felt called to shift my attention in another direction—towards restoring my body at a deeper level.

While energy work and other adjustments were invaluable, I needed to make some nutritional changes. I knew full well the benefits of eating high-quality organic food since I had been eating that way for most of my adult life. I have my first husband, John, to thank for introducing me to a more health-conscious diet at the age of nineteen. Alongside him, I learned more about our food and where it comes from and became a vegetarian. With this new knowledge, I drastically changed the way I was eating and continued on that track for over twenty years. However, I had gradually started eating chicken and fish after Noah was born. And after Claude's suicide, my diet had veered into a less healthy lane.

If I truly wanted to have a lasting effect on my health, I had to make changes to recalibrate my body on a cellular level.

Since I was already aware of the profound impact our diet can have on our health, it made perfect sense to start with that. I wanted to delve into not only eating more mindfully but also embracing the concept of food as medicine. It's funny—before my move to Colorado, one of the many intuitive snapshots I received was of me juicing on a regular basis. I loved that inspiring image and looked forward to the day when I would get myself into a juicing routine. Now, the time had surely arrived.

Based solely on my personal experience, I surmise that when we lose a loved one, we have the tendency to go in one of two directions. We can be in such emotional distress that we have no interest in feeding ourselves, resulting in weight loss. This was the case for me when my first marriage ended in divorce. Even though I remember repeatedly indulging, easily downing a pint of ice cream in one sitting, I still lost ten pounds. I was much thinner back then, so losing that weight was not at all a good thing. Friends would actually comment on how underweight I looked. With the help of an amazing therapist, I found my way into that new reality as a divorcée, eventually developing healthier eating habits.

On the flip side, another response can be to eat our way through grief. This is what I did after Claude died. I was so traumatized and engulfed by grief that I used food to soothe myself. This may sound funny, but I think my worst offense with food was when I became addicted to kettle corn during the first year after Claude died. I started with the small bags from Whole Foods, then graduated to the mega-bags from Costco. I sat in front of the TV and binge watched my favorite shows while chowing down on my crunchy, sweet, and salty drug of choice. It was an unhealthy combo for me, but I indulged for several months.

Besides my unhealthy snacking habits, I had begun to drink a bit more. Other than my rebellious teen years, I kept drinking alcoholic beverages to a minimum, and beer was my intoxicant of choice. Before Claude died, I would maybe have two beers per week, if that. After he died, alcohol became another thing that I relied on to soothe my pain during the first year or two. I would sometimes drink one per day—just enough to take the edge off. This may not sound like a lot, but being health conscious this was not ideal, not to mention those added pounds that beer is known for. When I noticed that my scale had predictably changed its tune I gradually weaned myself off my grief-ridden vices, calming any fears that my indulgence would have permanent consequences.

Before I had reached that stage, however, my therapist Catherine told me that "If that's the worst you're doing considering all that you have been through, it's really not that bad." I tend to be pretty hard on myself, and she knew that. She encouraged me to cut myself some slack. I guess it's all relative, isn't it? After that reminder, I initially chose to let myself do whatever I needed to get through each day, some of those things being healthy outlets and some things not so much. I gave myself full permission to do anything I could think of to nurture myself and ease the pain that lived inside me, whether it be with food, a walk in nature, a massage, a grief support session, a funny movie, crying, or screaming.

In Boulder, though, I was ready to move beyond immediate self-soothing and towards my long-term goal of healing.

A friend in Asheville told me about a woman named Ellen, who coaches people with her online 21-day food cleanses. I soon discovered that she had lost her husband to cancer, so she knew what I was dealing with. Because of this, I felt an added layer of understanding and support from her during our coaching calls. In addition to fine-tuning my diet, I knew I needed to lose the added pounds I'd put on after Claude died with my comfort eating.

I launched into the cleanse with full enthusiasm, learning new ways to eat and beginning to drop some weight in the process. Since I was feeling so much better, I continued eating that way. More importantly, I learned how to use food as medicine. I kept processed foods to a bare minimum, rarely eating gluten or dairy. I was juicing, making my own bone and vegetable broth, nut butters, and nut milks, and eating lots of soups and salads. Both Noah and I were taking full advantage of the local farmer's market that we are lucky enough to have available eight months out of the year. I thought I had been eating reasonably well before this, but these new improvements brought my diet to a whole new level. As I continued to eat more 'real' food, my body was loving it, and I was feeling stronger.

Nonetheless, as time passed, I felt there was still more that I needed to do. I explored various options to include in my medicinal toolkit and found out about a woman in town who helps detect and cleanse parasites, various latent viruses, and heavy metals from our bodies. I worked with her for about a year with significant results continuing to support my body's healing process. I felt emboldened by my progress and would continue on that path for years to come.

A cleanse of another sort was awaiting my nod of approval. When I bought our new townhome, I knew that updating our living space would be in our not-so-distant future. But I had no reserves for that sort of grueling undertaking after the move. After over a year of focusing on my health, I began hearing quiet murmurs of my intuition guiding me to take that next step of diving into the remodeling process. This would be the first time I had taken on a major house remodeling project without Claude. Thanks to my trepidation, I was resistant at first, but I repeatedly heard that I would be given the strength, and it was time to get that ambitious task behind us. I was told by my guides that if we could both be patient as we moved through that time, our new environment would help support what was to come by providing a peaceful and beautiful living space for both of us to dwell in.

This was yet another opportunity for me to trust in my inner guidance system. I knew it would be tough to get through, but I had gained enough ground with my health to withstand the taxing upheaval of the six-month process. Noah was all in, and I made sure to include him in many of the decisions of choosing the materials, with particular attention to his bathroom. Why not? It was a great learning experience, and with his exceptional aesthetic sense, I knew he would be an asset to the project. In addition, I wanted him to feel like he was a part of the process of creating our home together, just as we did when we moved in. We are vastly different people, but in matters of choosing home décor, we seem to match up rather nicely together. He and I even joined forces and did the painting ourselves.

With the flurry of the remodeling project behind us, we reveled in the peace, beauty, and harmony of our new living space. Our house had become our home, and putting our personal touches on it made all the difference.

I came to understand why I was guided first to rebuild my health and then to do the remodel. I was grateful that I listened to those inner promptings. Looking back, it all made perfect sense. We had cleansed the outdated energy that did not resonate with us, giving way to a feeling of rebirth. I felt empowered. Unlike many changes we are faced with over the course of our lifetimes, this change felt wonderful and liberating. We could now fully relax and feel a sense of accomplishment with another monumental project behind us.

The eternal nature of change had once again delivered on its promise while continuing to teach me to trust in the value of its essential characteristics. We can bend and flow with the essence of change, letting it have its way with us. Even when we resist, we inevitably discover the many gifts that it holds.

The trees were now fully stripped of their color, giving way to the winter months, and the cycles of hibernation were calling to me. I entered the cave for more deep healing and transformational work. Our new surroundings served perfectly as the nest I had hoped for. I was now ready to surrender, going inward as winter arrived.

*My heart is healing*
*& moving in the direction*
*of alignment with*
*eternal peace, love, and joy.*

# 15

# WISDOM

Continuing on my grief odyssey, I heard about an event that the Grief Support Network was sponsoring in the latter part of our first year in Boulder. This weekend workshop proved to be a powerful introduction to the circle of communal grieving. Since we are programmed in this society to grieve on our own, I found this notion intriguing.

The primary leading light of the workshop was Sobonfu Some. She was appointed by the elders of the Dagara tribe of Burkina Faso, West Africa as the "keeper of the rituals." Sobonfu taught worldwide before her passing in 2017. In hindsight, I feel grateful to have had the opportunity to spend time with this devoted wisdom keeper before she passed. Her purpose that weekend was to guide us through the time-honored methods of her native Grief Ritual. As a skilled way-shower, she held space along with our spirit helpers—namely, our ancestors. She explained that calling in our ancestral lineage is essential to finding our way to wholeness, peace, and acceptance.

Sobonfu shares that "Grieving is a soul-cleansing way to reclaim and recover our spirit. When we do not grieve, we stay in an unhealthy place and lose who we are, so it is very important to cry, to walk in nature, to express our grief so we can feel safe and sane once again."

I noticed the apparent difference between our western world and her place of origin as Sobonfu recounted stories of her people's ancient wisdom to our sizable group of seventy-five or so attendees. She told us that, in her culture, those who grieve were never set adrift or left to carry that weight alone. It was just the opposite. There were no judgments and no expected timeline for mourning. Instead, grief was seen as something natural that needed to be honored, highlighted, and engaged with by the entire village. If only that were true for all of us.

Thanks to the Grief Ritual, the weekend was at once intense and liberating. This was where she said we would 'do the work.' We were asked to bring flowers, red, blue and black fabric, candles, and photos of our lost loved ones and ancestors, including any meaningful mementos that felt important to share. We arranged them on two of the three ceremonial altars that we lovingly created together. The red altar was a place to honor our ancestors, while the blue was a place for prayers of self-forgiveness, filled with photos of the loved ones who would help us move through our grief and healing. The black was the grief altar lined with various nature and earth elements. In front of the grief altar were cushions and boxes of tissues.

Once the sacred ceremonial space was fully prepared, it was time to begin the Grief Ritual. We had set up a spot called "the village." This is where chanting, singing, drumming, and ceremonial rattles came into play. As the villagers, we all gathered there, moving to the altar that we felt most drawn to. The only rule was that nobody would go to the grief altar alone. Those who were at the grief altar would always be accompanied by one of the villagers to lend support either with a hand on the back, a hug, holding them while they cried, or someone simply bearing witness to their grief. It was an opportunity to be seen by 'a village' and held fully with our most tender and vulnerable emotions. Soon, the Grief Ritual was underway. The level of reverence, support, and unconditional love I experienced was beyond imagination. Each one of us had an untold story of grief that had clearly taken hold of our hearts. Our collective losses included family members, spouses, friends, pets, and romantic relationships. As I sat beside others in front of the grieving altar, ready and willing, I wasn't sure what to expect. Then, memories of finding Claude rose to the surface. Before I knew it, I was overcome with a cascade of feeling and flashbacks that I thought I had mostly put behind me. My tears were followed by screams and wailing. I didn't hold anything back, baring my still somewhat tattered heart for all to see.

I reached a new level of comprehension and appreciation while surrounded by other courageous souls showing up for their own grief, each with their unique declaration. Some were as undaunted and fully expressive as I was, while some were somber and restrained. It was all welcomed and respected, knowing that we each have our own distinctive expression and comfort levels in conveying our grief.

I experienced the fullness of what Sobonfu had described. The power of witnessing others in that once-in-a-lifetime setting and in turn being witnessed in my time of sorrow was a priceless gift. I wish we could all have an opportunity to come out of hiding and proclaim that which is silently binding our hearts and souls.

Just as Sobonfu says, "The Grief Ritual not only allows healing for the part of a person that has been hurt, but it's also a way of acknowledging that something else is being born in the Self … Grief is a doorway to healing. It is also a doorway to accessing one's power … and getting into one's creativity."

In his parallel universe, Noah was developing his *own* village of support. Through our newly forming grapevine, we happened upon Michael, a life coach who at the time specialized in working with families and teen groups. As a growing and impressionable high schooler, Noah was fortunate to have a role model during that key developmental period. Michael was known for his compassion and his ability to cultivate self-awareness. Through his programs, he empowered young ones to communicate more effectively and believe in themselves and their purpose in the world. I was over the moon with gratitude that Noah had this opportunity to work with a man of his caliber.

Still curious about the metaphysical world, Noah discovered the energy healing practice of Reiki through a fellow high school classmate. The Usui method, which originated in Japan, is a hands-on healing method used to transmit Universal Life Force Energy. Noah's classmate invited him to a teen Reiki group one Sunday afternoon led by a woman named Lisa. He continued attending her weekly gatherings to eventually earn his Reiki 1 and 2 certifications. As time passed, Lisa became one of his key teachers and advisors. She brought decades of experience in her varied healing modalities to him, and in her decidedly capable hands, he had found another guardian assisting him on his road of self-discovery.

Before long, I created my own connection with Lisa. I began with her astrology readings to acquaint myself with her work and was delighted to have discovered a true medicine woman with a heart of gold. She has vast knowledge and skills in various practices that I felt drawn to exploring further. Filled with enthusiasm, I added her as another trusted member of my healing team.

Lisa has been by my side ever since, assisting me to release outdated limiting beliefs and patterns as well as continue to heal my trauma and nervous system. As a result, I am able to sustain the work that is needed to let go of anything keeping me from truly loving and embracing all of who I am.

The progress I made through my work with Lisa reminds me of a letter that my mom wrote me after Claude and I got married. It highlights that vision she held for me beyond my fears and insecurities—the things that kept me small and held me back. It touched me so deeply I held on to the card all these years. To this day when I read it, I feel the depth of her love for me. The insight and wisdom that she wielded are noteworthy and relevant to my journey as a soul in this human experience.

She wrote:

*Try not to sell yourself short. We are all different; some are clever, some are smart, etc. You are perfect and a beautiful, loving person. Sensitive to others. Each morning, look for the beauty around you. Live each day to the fullest; the "powers" surround you. Think positive and give them a chance to work for you. Take each day at a time and realize the beauty of every moment. Realize all your dreams.*

Working with my constraining beliefs has been an ongoing awakening process. Losing Claude was a catalyst for growth in ways that I would have never envisioned for myself. Once you uncover and release one limiting belief or pattern, it's inevitable that you will uncover another, then another, and so on. It seems endless once you step on to the path of personal and spiritual growth in consciousness. But, it is well worth the time and effort to release those things that bind us, to fully awaken to the truth of who we are as sovereign creator beings.

Noah and I had been intensely engaging with our own individual healing journeys and just as we were beginning to feel grounded in our Boulder bubble, we heard the gut-wrenching news that Aztechan and her family would be moving to New York. Our reassuring and genuine family-like connection had been a comfort for those two fleeting years since moving to Boulder. Having that taken away so soon seemed inconceivable.

This unexpected development triggered another avalanche of grief that would take me months to work through. They left a considerable gap in the wake of their departure. Though this was clearly a different kind of loss, it was the ending of an irreplaceable chapter, and it hurt!

At that point, I was close to four years into my grieving process after Claude's suicide. This experience illuminated the true face of grief—it is opportunistic, lying in wait for just the right trigger. Grief has the full capacity to be awakened at any time, in any place. It comes in relentless cycles, and with each new round of piercing heartache, I began to think that maybe grief had hijacked my very existence. I wondered if I would ever live without it and the anguish that was so entwined with its core.

It took time for my heart to embrace the deeper spiritual understanding and see their move as being for the highest good for all concerned. Trusting that we are all guided to be exactly where we are meant to be helped to ease my pain. In the interim, I moved through a new season of loss. I was caught securely in the web of isolation and loneliness that comes with grief.

As I lay awake with insomnia one night, it came to me that there are two opposing aspects or factions breathing within me.

There is the wounded one who still grieves her loss of Claude. She expresses her needs when least expected. These include the need to cry and to be acknowledged, nurtured, and cared for. This part of me still feels the loss and misses her husband and the loving family that they created together. She is the one who lingers in grief. She is the one who remembers vividly what it felt like to find her beloved hanging in their attic. She is the one who has relived that moment hundreds of times, feeling the anguish in her heart and the enduring grief that followed.

In the darkness of the night, I came to the harsh realization that she will likely be with me for the rest of my life. However, those needs will likely lessen in their intensity over time.

Then, there is the other aspect. This is the part of me who celebrates all that has transpired since Claude has left because she has a broader understanding of our life's big picture. She is grateful that she has had the strength to stay alive through the many times when she wanted to give up with thoughts of suicide herself. She had to remind herself that there was a life worth living, that Noah still needed his mom. Reaching out for help from the angelic realm and her own mom's reminder from the other side that 'this too shall pass' surely kept her on this good red road.

She knows that there is really no death, only transitions to other realms that we humans have a limited capacity to understand. She sees that Claude's suicide has served an important purpose in their lives. Because of his departure, she and their son are living in a beautiful city that is more complementary to each of their individual needs and have created a life filled with purpose in spite of—and actually in response to—this loss. She understands that while this was unquestionably the most earth-shattering experience of her life, as a result, it has also been the most powerful. This loss encapsulates the greatest gifts and rewards along its tortured and arduous path. She is filled with gratitude for the dominion of this Widow's Moon.

Living with two opposing forces inside of me vying for control can have its challenges. However, they both hold valuable currency. She who carries the grief serves the purpose of feeling and processing her loss more earnestly as time passes. Without this, there can be no healing. On the other hand, she who holds the message of the truth of this life as a multidimensional being holds the key to understanding. Without this, there can be no hope for the future or forward momentum. Without this, she would ultimately be trapped in an inner world filled with suffering and hopelessness. Finding balance between these two is my life's quest.

I now have a more conscious understanding of what these parts of me need. This knowledge serves as a beacon moving through the twists and turns. I will listen to my dear wounded one with more tenderness when she needs my love and support. I will also listen to the wise one who celebrates this life with *all* that it contains and holds for us. Knowing that both sides are valid, I anchored into this new facet of understanding with a heightened sense of expectation and awareness.

From this epiphany, a new perspective on Aztechan's departure was born. I realized that I needed to be patient and surrender, allowing new friendships and people to be delivered into my life to ease the transition. This was a perfect opportunity to continue learning about faith in the natural flow of our lives.

Over time, I started to embrace changes with more clarity and less resistance, meeting each new change with curiosity instead of fear. I started to view major life transitions almost as a game. How would the Universe provide? How would the Universe fill in the gaps left by each new loss? Would I be dashed against the rocks of grief, or would I swim back to dry land and take the lessons with me?

Thankfully, I had my healing team in place for support and was able to access the strength of the light that resides within us all to ride out that dark cycle. It was reassuring to notice how four years of processing my grief had prepared me for this most recent orbital sequence of dark days. Like a waxing gibbous moon reaching its full splendor, this had ultimately been a time of healing, growth and emergence, and I wasn't going to let another loss hold me back from all that I had attained.

*I trust that*
*my heart knows*
*the path to healing.*

# 16

# ALIVE

A fter realizing how far I had come, it felt like the time had arrived to think about how I could assist others on this path. I couldn't shake the persistent call from the Divine nudging me to write a book detailing my journey following Claude's suicide. I distinctly heard that it was important to share what I had learned, lighting the way for those who grieve.

With her intuitive foresight, Marianne had previously advised me that my voice would be needed and that my role as a teacher would ultimately emerge. She said, "I think one day you will drop more fully into your clairaudience and use writing as a tool to help others."

On the one hand, the idea of being an author sounded preposterous. I proclaimed to my guides point-blank: "I am not a writer. If you want me to write this book you will have to show me the way and help me to hear the words that will be of service to my fellow travelers in need." On the other hand, it made perfect sense given my background in the healing arts and my propensity to be of service to the greater good. I decided that I would be open to the possibility, even if I had no idea of how things would unfold.

My guides evidently heard my request for assistance. As a complete neophyte in the world of writing, my initiation began with Marianne, who was teaching an online course that included an insightful exercise called the *Life Visioning Process*. This writing practice was created by Michael Bernard Beck of the AGAPE International Spiritual Center. At its core, the process uses writing prompts that invite us into the stream of universal consciousness. When we are able to bypass our usual mind-based stories and programs, we empower the guiding vision of our soul. In a way, it is no different than the process painting I learned to help myself accomplish a similar level of creative expression.

The more I practiced this process, the clearer the answers became. I received inner guidance from my True Self and those from the angelic realm who were by my side in the unseen world. Over time, I learned to trust that my guides imbued these writings with light and love, helping me to understand my life purpose and the truth of who I am beyond this human construct.

Since Claude's suicide, my entire existence has seemed to revolve around remembering this. The inner core of knowing has acted as my supreme guiding force and urged me to move forward each day. Because of this, it was no surprise to see what came through me during those visioning sessions and why Spirit led me to take that course with Marianne. What did surprise me was that these dispatches revealed such eternal wisdom that it was hard to ignore them as higher council, illuminated with reassurance and motivation.

What informed my decision to step on this writing path with even more resolve was the answer to this question posed to me by Marianne:

***What is the highest vision of my life?***

*To be the embodiment of Love, to share with others the grand scheme and true story of the Universe. To help others awaken to their own divinity and self-love. To be a beacon, sharing what I have learned through this academy of life through the path I have traveled. The times I have suffered. The joys I have manifested. All of it tells a story that will serve to inspire others on their own journeys, allowing them to feel safe and to feel hope that they, too, can awaken to their own divinity and truth of who they really are beyond this human condition. Beyond pain and suffering. Beyond this human-shielded awareness. Letting the veils be lifted to see the truth as it stands before each one of us, beyond time and space. The truth as it is revealed to each one's unique divination for this lifetime. With the unique gifts and abilities that all contribute to the whole.*

How could I say no to that? Every time I engaged with this process it felt as if I were opening a treasure trove of glistening gemstones. Each holds such potentiality and profound levels of spiritual awareness that I wouldn't have accessed otherwise.

An auspicious and altogether unexpected outcome resulted from this *Life Visioning Process.* I began to find myself engaging in a journaling practice that would evolve into automatic writing. The self-determining messages that emerged continued to light my way, guiding me with their divine illuminations.

Through automatic writing, I had several encounters with Claude sharing reflections on his death and his thoughts on my continued life without him. In fact, Claude was actually an exceptional writer. We'd talked many times over the years about the book he might someday write. Thanks to that fact, I find my own journey as a writer rather interesting and ironic. I often wonder if he is behind this, or at the very least a part of my ethereal writing squad, softly whispering into my ear.

The transmissions from Claude in particular felt moving, helping me rise to a newly updated level of peace and clarity about the way he died:

*Our relationship has changed. It is transforming as you write this. You were once my wife, but no more. You are now my soul partner. We are still in union with our son and will always be a part of one another, but you must let me go.*

*You don't need to hold on for dear life anymore. It's not necessary. Please know this: I am okay. All is well where I am. You are not to blame for my decision to commit this act. It was mine alone to decide to exit this way. You were not responsible for my actions and you couldn't have done a thing to stop me.*

*Please know this: You are allowed to be happy. It's ok to live with joy again. Please laugh. Remember how much it meant for me to make you laugh and smile. If not for you, would you please do this for me?*

*Let the heavy barge go, let it drop from your shoulders. It does not belong to you anymore. You will feel so much lighter, which is what I intended when I left—to set you two free!*

*ONE, TWO, THREE … LET GO NOW and jump into FREEDOM! Take a BIG BREATH and LET GO! Let me go, and let this heavy barge go. I know you can do it. It may take a little while to drop all the pieces, so take your time if you need to, but know you won't be losing me. You will be gaining me in a new way.*

*You know who you truly are. Please open your beautiful angel wings and fly, fly, my friend, it is your birthright!*

I could feel his loving presence and the depth of his impassioned appeal. Though it was liberating on a certain level to hear this, it would indeed take some time for me to patiently "drop all those pieces."

Nevertheless, these transmissions served their intended purpose—to usher me to the seat of my soul. There, my unique foundational template resides, waiting to be drawn upon. After continuing my writing practice for several months, I received the guidance that I should start a blog to share my thoughts and experiences through grief.

Since I trusted this inner voice implicitly, I knew it was officially time to come out of the shadows. Knowing how exposed I would feel, this was a frightening and risky proposition, but I heard that this would help me gain confidence with my writing. It was an opportunity to develop my voice.

When envisioning what my blog might look like, I knew I wanted to include images so that readers could engage with the healing qualities of nature. I had been accumulating photos on my morning walks with devotion, and I would now have the perfect platform to share my images.

My goal was to 'go live' on the fourth anniversary of Claude's suicide. After several weeks, I had created my blog site entirely on my own to reach that self-imposed deadline. I felt proud of my accomplishment, and I knew that Claude would have approved wholeheartedly. I began writing my posts as a complete novice with utmost terror every time I clicked 'Publish.' Despite this, my resolve remained unbroken as I stayed on task week after week, month after month.

Once I got past the initial fears, I enjoyed the challenge of writing those posts and sharing my story. However, given the subject matter, I had to go into my traumatized memory banks, retracing all of the factual information, recounting the timeline, and of course bringing to the surface all of the harrowing emotions of that inconceivable episode in my life. I held no illusions that it would be an easy task; nevertheless, it took its toll on me.

A year into blogging, I found myself sliding into depression and daily anxiety. I had misplaced my joy, my motivation to write, and the desire to keep moving forward. My grief felt heavy once again. After all, telling and crafting an account of my tender and personal grieving process was an intense experience. So finally, I gave myself permission to take a break, creating the space I needed to process all of this. Maybe then I would find a path to finding my mislaid light again.

I have learned about depression in my own life experiences and through watching Claude's descent. Sometimes, depression takes root when we have become sidetracked due to fear and resistance. When we are living in fear and out of alignment with our souls' decrees, we are more vulnerable to succumbing to the swirling waves of depression. We may feel stuck in the calm eye of the storm that threatens to sweep us away.

It's in that place where our souls' directives get diverted that we forget to listen to our inner guidance, or maybe we simply ignore it, lost in the storm with no clear path ahead.

As time passed, something continued to feel off. I was confined by my hindering emotions, and I knew it was time to start shifting gears. With support from one of my trusted healers, I found my way back to the song of my soul. At one point, I stopped and asked myself, *What am I NOT doing that my soul desires and requires of me?*

The answer was simple and to the point: *You need to get back to your blog and begin your book.*

I heard this message loud and clear, and I felt a sense of joyfulness and almost giddy excitement at the thought of writing again. Feeling this was always an indication of truth for me, so I knew I was on the right track.

Yet despite this impassioned guidance, I remained temporarily bewitched by my habitual and outdated blueprint of anxiety, depression, and grief. This is a very old pattern that has played like an aggravating skip on a record album, coming back around and around every time I thought it had left for good. It became clear to me that it was time to switch albums.

When we recognize that we are not actually pledged to and bound by our stories—that we have the authority to transmute them—we give rise to the expanse of the soul's expression. We have reached a powerful and transformational period on this planet. This time is calling upon each one of us to be courageous enough to step forward, come out of hiding, and venture into the light to share our medicine with the world. We all came here with an important purpose. We just need to listen to the reminders.

Maybe it was Claude or perhaps one of my angelic comrades who sent me another reminder of the importance of my light, my life. I was driving in my car on an early January day, the beginning of my fifth year since Claude's suicide. Listening to Pandora Radio, a favorite Pearl Jam song came on. It is called "Alive."

I listened to Eddie Vedder's expressive, soulful voice and heartfelt ability to deliver a lyric as he sang the words "I'm still alive." This main stanza of the song felt like a divinely appointed prescription that I couldn't ignore. It circled through my mind as a mantra weaving its seductive tones throughout the next several days.

The message was loud and clear: *Although Claude is gone, I am still alive! I am still here to get on with my life, to get on with what I came here to do. I have a mission just like everyone else here on this planet. Losing someone we love does not change that. In fact, it can actually help reshape and solidify the course of our lives moving forward.*

I had a stark realization: although I had created some incredible things in my life since Claude's suicide, there was for a long time an undercurrent pulling me down and holding back my truest joy and happiness. I was still carrying some sticky unresolved pieces of that heavy burden from the barge Claude had described in his transmission.

Hearing these dynamic lyrics helped me to expose the concealed belief that I would be betraying his memory if I were to *really* embrace a joy-filled life. How could I do that considering how he left us? Claude's messages were right on. It's no wonder that he tried his best to help me understand this. He was no longer suffering, so why should I be?

The part of me that lost her life in that attic when I found him needed this wake-up call. She needed to be resurrected once and for all. Though her beloved was gone and she would never be the same, she needed to understand that this was actually her greatest gift. Without her loss, the woman writing these words would not exist. The wisdom gained would not exist. Her life as she knows it would not exist.

After hearing that song, I felt inspired to stop living with guilt. I had grown so tired of carrying that part of the weight. I was opened to the possibility of being breathed by life in a whole new way. With this, the activation of freedom Claude had talked about was slowly being delivered into this new reality.

I was grateful to have restored excitement about living this life. It genuinely did feel like I was coming 'alive' again. Sure, there were those inevitable bouts of the timeworn, yet familiar resistance to change bubbling to the surface. It took me some time to process this shift and my understanding of how I could *truly* re-create my life. There was an adjustment period, a gentle and gradual recalibration of the old vs. the new. Parts of myself rose up in opposition, diligently trying their best to hold me back and keep me safe with the status quo. Despite this, my resolve would lead me to secure a purpose-driven life.

Devotion to writing in service to others came to the forefront as something that my soul longed for. This sense of purpose became central to my healing journey and is what brought these words to your eyes.

*I joyfully embrace
the light of my soul,
as it guides me
to my new life purpose.*

# 17

# ALCHEMY

Just after losing Claude, I'd felt as though the grounding cord linking me to the center of the earth had been cut. Residing in this space, it was as if the Universe had abruptly confiscated the fragments of my life and replaced them with something completely unrecognizable.

In the aftermath of a loss, we are charged with finding our individual ways to reconfigure those fragments. Simply put, our lives are transforming and energetically recalibrating. In the meantime, we find ourselves in a state of overwhelm and disorientation. We wonder, *who are we now?*

Yet our adjustments create the revised blueprint of our new reality moving forward. It's important to tune in and listen to our inner wisdom for clues on how to navigate this inner shift. It takes time, but when there is a willingness to say yes to our souls, there is hope, there is light, and there is love. We are full of potential.

After soaking in my own restorative alchemical bath for five years, my health and energy levels had vastly improved. My essence felt more radiant, as if it had been burnished and buffed. I knew without question that the most difficult times were behind me.

Noah sensed this transformation, too, so he began circling me and insisting that we adopt a new dog. Our poodles were no longer with us, so there was a vacancy that, in his eyes, needed to be filled. Despite my hesitancy, once I was under Noah's unshakable, silver-tongued spell, I was a goner. Before I knew it, we had launched full-on into doggie acquisition mode.

After a few unsuccessful tries, we welcomed a dear 11-pound all-white terrier mix from a local rescue organization into our home. Not long after we got our little one, I ran into a neighbor who happened to be an intuitive consultant. We had a brief conversation, and as we parted ways, she paused and looked back. She said with supreme authority, "You know, she was sent to you." I was a bit taken aback by this direct and unexpected message. Yet I had to admit it felt that way to me as well. Our puppy's soul seemed like it was from another world. Because of that, I named her Lyra (after the constellation). Her all-white appearance unquestionably amplifies the notion that she is one of my angelic helpers.

Lady Lyra, my muse, has blessed us with her devotion and unconditional loving presence ever since. Between the lake and the trails, she and I have put in a lot of miles together. She satisfies many elements of my life that were missing. Noah's inspiration was right on—that void in my life sorely needed filling.

As I leaned into better emotional and physical health with Lyra at my side, I started reflecting on how I might want to celebrate my approaching sixtieth orbit around the sun. I considered the importance of beginning the new decade in an optimistic and meaningful way.

Claude's conspicuous absence at this particular birthday occasioned a now-familiar disorientation. On my fortieth birthday, Claude adeptly and lovingly coordinated a surprise party at our home in Pacifica, California. For my fiftieth, we took a family trip up to Washington state. Growing old together and sharing many more birthdays was one of our greatest desires. However, the universe had another plan for us. Reminiscing and pining for an unattainable past brought me to unavoidable anguish. But thankfully, I was now securely on the other side of the darkest turbulent waters. Yes, I still had ripples of grief wash upon my shore, but they were far less impactful than they had been.

Up until that point, the thought of traveling had felt like it would be too taxing on my system. I had remained in Colorado for three years to focus on my healing, but I now felt ready to venture out again. After weighing the options, I decided to celebrate my birthday in Asheville—the first stop on my new travel itinerary.

Why would I want to open those old wounds? In actuality, I don't think those particular wounds had completely healed. That meant I needed to face my fears and reclaim what was once my 'special place' in the present. I imagined reconnecting and visiting with people that I loved in a part of the country that once brought me peace and endless joy.

My inner knowing called on me to heal and retrieve another handful of lost pieces. If not now, when? This was the year that I would cross over the threshold, emerging into the next decade of my life. There was a potent invitation to clear that which may hinder my advancing momentum.

Gwen was still living in Nashville at the time. She and I decided to come full circle as travel companions. I envisioned our trip to Asheville as a joyful reunion and celebration of our mutual sixtieth birthdays, which happened to be only two months apart.

My birthday fantasy was to have a ceremony out in nature anchoring in our rite of passage. I knew that one of Marianne's specialties is performing earth-based rituals for varying life transitions, so it made perfect sense for me to reach out to her. Without hesitation, she agreed to officiate. I was thrilled to know that she would be there to celebrate and honor us with the purity of her soulful and loving presence. My curiosity heightened when she shrewdly hinted that she had the perfect location in mind.

The fact that it was the month of May, my favorite of them all, enhanced the delight of the moment at hand. Yes, it holds the date of my birth, but it's so much more than that to me. May is an exuberant time of rebirth. The natural world reemerges, surrounding us with popping flowers and exploding spring green in a joy-filled rollick. After living in a dry and less verdant climate in Colorado, it was a welcome color bath.

Marianne drove us along the picturesque Blue Ridge Parkway, winding our way through the Appalachian Mountains. She told us that these mountains were some of the oldest in our country and hold within them the ancient wisdom of our dear Gaia or Earth Mother. I smiled inside, noting that this was most assuredly divinely appointed. I was glad I said yes to this!

We approached our destination with eager anticipation. After gathering our things and hiking on a trail through the forest, we reached our transcendental paradise. Our senses were instantly consumed by a captivating, otherworldly waterfall that was the embodiment of the sacred. With its unmistakable majesty, it did not disappoint. There wasn't a soul in sight. The outside world was put on hold as we entered a private, enchanted sanctuary populated by nature spirits and fairies.

The intention for this ceremony was to honor the potentiality of the life transition that both Gwen and I were embarking upon. We also sought to release those things that no longer served us while inviting and embracing all things that would assist us as we moved forward. What a remarkable gift to share this holy occasion with these two extraordinary medicine women who I love deeply; each in their own way is a teacher and spiritual alchemist. Both were an integral part of my healing, transformation, and growth while traversing my path through grief. We all walked away from that day feeling full and satiated with the potentiality and sweetness of Spirit.

Two days later, Gwen suggested that she and I do a second ceremony to access the potency of those Appalachian waters once again. I was all in and knew of an easily accessible waterfall on another portion of the Blue Ridge Parkway that would serve our intended purpose. The purpose of this ceremony was forgiveness and releasing any latent layers around Claude's suicide—forgiving him for leaving us the way he did and forgiving myself for not being able to save him. This is one of the areas of challenge for those of us who've had a loss by suicide. Though this was something that I had already spent quite a bit of time grappling with, forgiveness is an ongoing process of releasing those accumulated layers of pain and struggle. She suggested we use rose petals this time, and I was elated to find some of 'our' purple roses at a local grocery store.

We drove up another winding road with inexhaustible breathtaking views around every turn until we arrived at our next cascading fairyland. Together, Gwen and I climbed up the path and found just the right spot to begin. I took a breath and planted my feet firmly on two adjacent boulders, straddling the cool running water flowing beneath me. As I stood there, Gwen had me voice the prayers of forgiveness. We each offered the rose petals to the waters. Quiet tears fell as I witnessed them gently slide over the rock formations, disappearing from view. This was another powerful expression of love and the art of letting go. Knowing this was yet another rung on that ladder to wholeness, my heart felt a little lighter.

Each day of our week-long trip was choreographed, packed with places and activities that filled me with joy and fed my soul. Some of the highlights included dining at my favorite restaurants in Asheville and Black Mountain, hiking in the Appalachians, visiting with dear friends, and receiving a heavenly hot stone massage in a Himalayan salt-lined room with Michael, the massage therapist who was on my healing team years before. I also bought a new bounty of stones and two new rings at our all-time favorite rock and mineral shop.

I have long been drawn to the spiritual and metaphysical properties of stones. If you were to visit my home, you would see them scattered throughout. I also wear them daily. While there are many books and websites on the subject, I use my intuition to guide me to the most beneficial stones. Once you have crystals or stones, you can use them to meditate and energize drinking water. Likewise, you can carry them throughout the day or place them with you as you sleep.

On that trip, I picked up more moonstone, which I wear often. It's known for embodying the divine feminine, enhancing intuitive abilities, and assisting with the ebb and flow of the cycles in our lives as well as the cycles of the moon. Rose quartz is another lovely addition that can be used for self-compassion, love, and balancing tender emotions while grieving.

While I'm happy to have labradorite, selenite, amazonite, aquamarine, and turquoise (among others) as reminders of this trip, without a doubt, the most treasured aspects are the memories of time spent in the magical mountain hideaways with Marianne and Gwen.

As it turned out, being back in Asheville felt surreal—familiar, yet unfamiliar. The old and new worlds were colliding and recalibrating. However, my goal of creating new and favorable memories was fulfilled. I couldn't have asked for a more heart-centered and enjoyable birthday. Once again, it was gratifying to note that I had listened to the call of my soul with its eternal clear-sightedness guiding my way.

A few nights later, I was back in my comfy bed in Boulder. I felt a renewed sense of purpose and enthusiasm; I was ready to start a new chapter. Buzzing with this energy, I descended the stairs heading down to the main floor of my home and, all at once, lost my footing.

Abruptly, I found myself slipping down the carpeted stairway as if I were sliding out of the birth canal into my new life. Thankfully, I was not injured except for some minor bruising and aches. But, wow! That was a rough entry into a day that felt so full of promise just minutes before. I am not prone to falling or accidents in general, so I wondered, *why the heck did this happen?*

Later that morning, it got even more interesting. I discovered that my car battery was dead. And just three days after that, I came down with a pretty intense cold. Needless to say, this was not the auspicious beginning I was intending—*or was it?*

I wrote this in my journal the first couple of days of my illness. One entry read:

*I am in an emotional quagmire of anger, grief, anxiety, fear, agitation, and self-judgment, yet still there is gratitude. Is all of this the result of what I asked for during my two healing ceremonies in Asheville? My body aches; my heart aches. I can't think straight. What's this all about? Why do I feel that I will burst if I don't do or say something? Is this what transformation looks like?*

*I know from past experiences that the cleansing process can sometimes be pretty messy before you reach the other side. With all the changes I have gone through, you would think I would be used to this. You would think that I would trust that this is all just part of my healing process.*

These occurrences serving to slow me down all pointed to the fact that I needed some quiet time for rest and renewal after all that was stirred up during my adventures. As with all opportunities for growth, patience is key. I have learned that it takes time for these changes to become fully integrated, embodied, or alchemized.

As I hoped and expected, things evened out. So, after a few weeks, I was ready to go on another excursion. Later in the summer, I visited Aztechan and her family who had moved from New York to Southern California. I treated myself to a vacation rental close to where they were living which was within walking distance to the beach. On this trip, it was time to reclaim a connection to the Pacific coast. It had been four years since the boat ceremony where I honored Claude.

Looking back, a good portion of my coastal history with Claude took place on the waters of Northern California. The most notable jaunt in the southern part of the state was in Carlsbad, where we granted Noah his longtime childhood wish of going to Legoland.

Because of our mutual desire to be by the water, we did our best to make sure we spent our family trips at the ocean whenever possible.

Being on the beach again with Aztechan was pure nirvana. We went there daily, taking long, delightfully calming walks. I had forgotten how blissful it is to stroll barefoot on the beach with the moist sand and the cool refreshing waves caressing my feet. Each day felt like a sublime interlude—a time to pause, soak it all in, and contemplate my very existence.

One day, I sat there lazing on my beach chair, my feet buried in the soft warm sand while I watched the waves glistening in the sun. I couldn't help but see momentary holographic reflections of my past. Amidst the waves, I saw images of Claude and Noah, father and son, having the time of their lives. Little did we know in the innocence and simplicity of those moments what the future held.

I found myself longing for him. Grief steadily reawakened in my heart, leaving my eyes soaked with tears. But staying with those feelings, an awareness began to emerge. I was able to affirm to myself just how far I had come since Claude's suicide. Yes, grief was still in the mix, but it was also important to note that I had genuinely healed in innumerable ways over those five years.

I arrived back in Colorado with the realization that what held true for Claude held true for me: I need the water just as much as I need the stability of the mountains. What served as a lifeline to his soul mirrored my own need. After that trip, I pledged to visit the coast at least once per year.

I had now reclaimed the seashore for myself, creating new memories just as I did during my trip to Asheville. With more steps came more layers of restoration.

In addition to being out in the natural world, I recommitted to my other lifelines. These include having a home that is surrounded by beauty inside and out, including a space for flower gardens with fountains to bring a soothing sound frequency and moisture into this dry climate. Also essential are creativity, healthy food, time with friends and family, and of course my sweet little canine companion, Lyra. Finally, my trusted healers and guides are needed to lift me up into the light. All these elements serve as continual reminders of who I am beyond my grief and this human form.

*The divine energies of
light & transformation
are guiding me
through my grief.*

# 18

# LOVE

I was a proud mama as I watched Noah reach two consecutive milestones, once again without his dad. He emerged into adulthood with his eighteenth birthday, and soon thereafter, graduated from high school. Given all that my son had faced, it was a relief knowing that he was not just intact but becoming a well-adjusted young man.

Instead of going right to college after graduation, Noah opted for taking a gap year. He clearly needed a breather, but still wanted to further his personal growth. While most kids have the desire to go off and discover the world, he had his own ideas. He wanted to travel inward, setting a strong foundation for the years to come.

Knowing that he held this mindset, I introduced him to Brendon Burchard's online courses. He was soon fixated on learning all he could and even worked with one of Brendon's coaches for a more personal approach. Through it all, he deepened his knowledge of the habits that enable success.

Brendon's courses helped Noah assemble a daily routine incorporating yoga, working out, meditation, piano, healthy eating, and cooking among other valuable tools for living a purposeful life. By the end of the year, he was feeling well-prepared for continuing his higher education at CU Boulder as a psychology major. We both felt gratified by his accomplishments; he was clearly keeping his promise to make his dad proud.

As Noah was well into his second year at college, I was working on the first draft of this book. I started hearing those small, faint voices from within, urging me to begin taking steps to open my heart to romantic love again. As usual, they got so loud that I had to take action.

Over those past six years since Claude's suicide, my priority had been to heal from the emotional trauma and loss on all levels. Due to the intensity, determination, and focus needed for that task, there really wasn't any room for a relationship. As a result, I hadn't sought the company of a man to soothe my wounds during this significant time of growth and transformation.

Those seemingly endless years of tending to my grief and healing had delivered me to a purposeful moment where I heard: *YOU are the one you have been waiting for.*

This prompt from the Universe signaled a readiness and ripening. I felt assured that my dedication had actually paid off. I had reached a new level of empowerment, growth, and understanding on this journey.

I am grateful for that solo season of the Widow's Moon, the relevance of which cannot be overstated. It gave me space and time to grow in innumerable ways. Amongst other lessons, I learned to love and value myself in the absence of a partner's reflecting love.

Even so, it seemed that it was time to shed a layer of my outworn widow's skin. Yes, I would always be a widow, carrying those inner and outer gifts gained, but it was apparent that this release was stimulating a rebirth into another moon phase.

I wanted to move in the direction of sharing my life again with a significant other. It wasn't that I was looking for someone to complete me. In certain ways, I felt more strength within myself than ever before. Nevertheless, I longed for physical loving touch, companionship, and to love and be loved in the way that can only be expressed with a life partner. I also knew that an intimate relationship can be one of our greatest teachers. With all that I had learned, I was ready to take that next step in my personal and spiritual development.

Even Claude agreed. Through my automatic writing with him, I heard this:

> *You need to heal so that you can allow for a loving man to come into your life. I want to see you happy and loved again. I see him; he is a special soul. You will be happier than you ever thought possible. PLEASE my sweet, I LOVE you dearly, and I want you to be happy and healthy. You MUST do this. You are brave, you have come so far, and you have so much to offer. I know this. You were a gift to me all those years we were together. Don't forget that you are pure love and kindness. Simply be yourself. You are ENOUGH just as you are.*

Though I maintained this as a future possibility, at first I held back. The thought of trusting and being vulnerable with another felt frightening. However, I noticed that my choice to remain single had become a comfortable and safe habit. Self-limiting beliefs and thoughts kept me suspended in fear. Sometimes I wondered, *how could I ever unwrap the protection I've fashioned around my heart? How could I ever trust my heart with another?* It would feel too risky, knowing how it can *all* be taken away in an instant. Sometimes I asked myself, *how could someone love me again after all that I had gone through?* Was I too damaged for someone to love and devote themselves to me?

With the conscious awareness of these beliefs and others, I could lovingly attend to them. It would require complete surrender to yet another expression of this Widow's Moon—to the unknown and the unfolding potentiality of the love that I was being guided to.

This passage came to me one day as I sat overlooking the lake:

> *When we have suffered a major loss, the tendency is to keep a barrier around our hearts for fear of receiving another crushing*

*blow. But the truth is that while this method is effective at keeping us in the illusion of safety, we are only hurting ourselves. When we open our hearts to love again, we have the ability to heal a thousand wounds.*

This strategy of "maintaining a barrier around my heart" had been an effective one. But all things considered, it felt like it had become an outdated program. I understood why I had created this now-defunct protective mechanism; however, I no longer needed that line of defense.

In truth, through all of the sculpting and recasting, I have emerged redefined. The woman I am today would not exist without these trials and tribulations.

The time had arrived to take steps towards unwinding and unraveling my fears. One such step was to nurture self-love. I began to sense that one of the most loving things I could do for myself was to unlatch not only my heart but also my imagination, essentially granting myself permission to *believe* that I am deserving and worthy of having the love that I desire. Beyond that, I could maintain the faith that it is indeed possible to find love again.

Over the years, I had been learning more about self-love and believing that I am *enough,* as Claude so lovingly reinforced. Each in their own way, Gwen, Marianne, Lisa, and even Eeris helped me release many of the blockages relating to romantic love and the barriers to loving myself unconditionally.

It's been an ongoing process to love myself *right where I am.* This entails accepting my human wounds, messiness, and vulnerabilities, all without judgment or the feeling that I need to be 'fixed.' This human condition is a challenging quest that requires our dedicated conscious awareness. Sure, we want to heal and transform, yet we must also honor our unresolved emotional wounds and entanglements, knowing that those aspects of ourselves are just as worthy of compassion and love. In addition, we must acknowledge that the miraculous bodies we inhabit are sacred containers meriting our loving care.

In one of our sessions, Gwen suggested this Law of Attraction practice:

*Allow myself to be in LOVE with ME! When I am in LOVE with ME, the other person can reflect back what I'm feeling. In other words, when we are vibrating at the frequency of love, we attract love.*

With this in mind, I started a practice of gazing at myself in the mirror before going to sleep. Each night, I look into my eyes, recognizing the brilliant divine light and love within. I smile, I touch my face, and say *I love you; you are beautiful.* I noticed how this simple practice can shift my energy in an instant. I discovered I was on to something when I stumbled upon Louise Hay's book called *Mirror Work*, which goes into more detail with these exercises.

Gwen also recommended that I allow myself to feel and imagine what I want a relationship to feel like (i.e., *I want my relationship to feel safe, joyful, loving, nurturing, and supportive*).

Gwen had been telling me for years that she saw me finding a partner through online dating. To say I was resistant is an understatement. I came from a generation where meeting men had always been more organic and natural. Just the thought of being on those dating sites made me want to run and hide. I thought that surely there must be another way. But sadly, times have changed, and this seemed to be the best way forward. I knew what I wanted, so I finally gave in. Being a person of action, I went into full-on manifestation mode.

I shouldn't have been surprised by the result. As if right on cue, once I said yes to the Universe, an online course about attracting your soulmate was delivered to my inbox. Arielle Ford and Claire Zammit created an online course called *The LOVE Codes*. This program was perfect for me, and the message couldn't have been clearer, yet I hesitated. My mind with its full arsenal of fear-based reasoning was overriding my intuition. I thought about it for days, analyzing and telling myself all of the reasons I shouldn't do it. Finally, as the deadline for signing up approached, I allowed my True Self to take command of the situation. I clicked on the signup button with relief, and I never looked back.

Once I had the time to review the comprehensive curriculum in its entirety, I made the determination that I would like to finish within 3-4 months. I envisioned signing up for online dating soon after that. At long last, I had a plan.

It was an emotional project packed with assignments for processing past relationships and getting clear on what I was looking for in a new relationship. For example: what were my top three must-haves and deal breakers? Echoing Gwen's suggestion, how did I want my relationship to feel? There were instructions for setting up a love altar, manifesting meditations, and other essential tools and checklists.

Thankfully, they also had modules dedicated to helping with constructing my online profile, which I was absolutely clueless about. As I moved through each course module, I found myself being bolstered and encouraged. I started feeling like I could actually do this. Was I still scared? Absolutely!

I spent days writing and re-writing my profile following their system. It took some time, but eventually, I got my photos together. It wasn't perfect, but it was a place to start. I set my sails with the wind behind me in honor of Claude's wishes and was on my way to the new world of online dating.

I felt relieved on the one hand, as I had lots of men contact me, so I guess I had done something right. But for the most part, I wasn't interested. I felt discouraged. I did go on a few dates with some very nice men before I met the one with who I would choose to move forward. This all happened rather quickly within a month of going live.

This man had many of the qualities that I outlined, plus we hit it off right away. I even felt the way I wanted to feel with him. I remember thinking, *could it really be this easy?* He was a kind man who I enjoyed, we had a lot in common, and I felt safe and comfortable with him.

Despite that, it became clear after several months that a friendship would be a better fit for me. Fortunately, he agreed to those terms, enabling us to maintain our relationship at that level.

Several months later, I met another man who I truly thought was the guy for me. We had a loving, magical connection from the start and were aligned in ways that were mind-blowing. We seemed to have it all. But unfortunately, he had come to me with unresolved pain around his own heart and a cancer diagnosis. To top it all off, COVID-19 rocked our world. The cards seemed stacked against us despite our undeniable soul connection. After many months of hoping things would shift in our favor, it didn't happen.

In my fantastical fairy-tale mind, I wanted to end this book with a "Happily Ever After." I wanted to tell you that my storybook man had arrived and that we are deliriously happy to this day. Though that is not the case *yet*, I want to reinforce that this is all a process.

Clearly, I still have some of my own resistance to work through. Maybe I wasn't as ready as I thought I was. In the big picture, the lesson may have been more about being brave enough to put myself out there despite my lingering fears. I don't want to give the impression that I was not deeply disappointed and saddened. I spent much time processing and grieving each of these losses. It's all part of this risky business of love.

Luckily, I am tenacious by nature, so for me, it's all worth it. If I had not taken a chance, I would not have had the wonderful experiences that I shared with these men. Each was so different individually, yet they each allowed me to open my heart and grow. Through their eyes, I learned even more about appreciating and loving myself.

At the heart of this, these encounters have anchored in the essential truth: the most important relationship I have is with myself. All else revolves around the practicing of loving ME—both my human and Higher Self, holding all of their glory and distinguishing threads of light and dimension.

It takes a tremendous amount of courage and strength to imagine putting ourselves in a vulnerable position again. It can feel much easier to stay single in the perceived zone of safety. Many of us may even get trapped in the inner dialog that says, "I could never find *that* kind of love again." But what if this is just another story that we are telling ourselves? What if we could find something even better than what we have dreamed of? What if this is one of the many gifts that are available to us if we are open to receiving?

Maybe, too, our departed loved ones are working behind the scenes to bring things into perfect alignment so that we can absolutely find love again when the time is right. Recognizing this and doing the inner work is essential to preparing for this union, especially when we have been so deeply wounded.

Unfortunately, there are no guarantees. Our lives are filled with insecure and edgy moments. We may find ourselves in the position of heartbreak and disappointment untold times. I know I have. After all, we are all on loan to one another, and all things by nature are impermanent. The fact that we may be bold enough to throw our hats into the ring regardless of this is admirable.

We must remember that we are worthy of love and that we are enough just as we are. Despite the outcome, we have gained something that is profoundly valuable as we step out into this new uncharted territory.

Remember, when all is said and done, it's about the journey and what we are learning along the way. With every lesson, we put ourselves more closely in alignment with what we truly desire from this divine dance called life. We can choose to invite love and celebrate our courageous hearts knowing that in the process, we may find something truly extraordinary. Life is a collection of defining moments if we are able to notice, listen, and participate.

Gazing back through my grieving years through my revised perspective on widowhood, it has been a wonder-filled journey. As I look forward to finding my new beloved, I see that the potent promise of this Widow's Moon has already been fulfilled. I have learned to be true to myself and in the process feel complete and whole again. I am more self-aware and more ready than ever for love and to be the shining light I came here to be. I have unwrapped my courageous heart and I now know that I am worthy of love. So are you.

*I am worthy of love just as I am.*
*I choose to love & nurture myself.*
*I have a courageous heart.*

# EPILOGUE

## Grief is Like the Moon

When I began my grief journey, I had no idea my heart would continue to ache so profoundly months or even years after Claude's suicide. Following my mom's transition from this life, I went through a grieving process that magically vanished on the one-year anniversary of her passing. Why or how this could have happened still remains a mystery to me. But as if on cue, I switched gears, stepping into another reality. From that day forward, I felt lighter, as if a dark cloud had been lifted. Since I had this model of how I grieved her loss, I naively concluded that something along those lines would follow in the aftermath of Claude's passing.

As you know from reading, this has not been the case. The consensus seems to be from those who have lived with a significant loss that the pain never really does fully go away. It may take many years to process, maybe even a lifetime. In fact, the seemingly endless rotations of grief can sometimes feel even more emotionally overpowering as time passes. Although grief is sometimes gentler, it can wear on our psychological well-being over time. You start to wonder if you will ever be free of the pain that continues to knock on your door day after day.

Even as I am invited to dance with these rhythms of grief, my attention must always circle back to surrounding myself with loving kindness. I have learned that having these feelings is not a sign that something is wrong with me or that I am broken beyond repair. They are not negative or bad; they simply need a space to be heard and acknowledged. These moments require our deepest love and reverence. Our human hearts are fragile, yet it's important to remember they are stronger than we can fathom.

While caught in these troubled waters, compassionate nurturing care is key to softening the impact. We can always call on the light within to guide us through the darkness, which brings us the solace that we seek. Two of my mom's favorite expressions "this too shall pass" and "it's always darkest before the dawn" are timeless reminders that all things and feelings are transient in nature. I can say with certainty that this is the absolute truth. My feelings always shift, and when they do, I am free once again to move forward with my renewed sense of Self. Patience and willingness are required to ride this out time after time.

I have heard it said again and again that we experience grief much like the ebb and flow of the ocean's waves, intermittently touching our hearts with its bitterness. It can sometimes be felt as a gentle ripple, and sometimes it even flattens us like a tidal wave out of nowhere.

Though I have experienced these unstoppable waves of grief in all their splendor and variations, for me this analogy implies that there are times when grief leaves us.

Through my intuitive guidance, an alternate perspective on the nature of grief was shown to me. I was shown an image of the moon. In this image, the moon represents our grief. I saw that our grief never really leaves us as the 'ebb and flow' scenario would suggest. Just as the moon is always present, despite its level of illumination, so is our grief. The moon goes through its cycles just as our grief does. We have times when our grief is in full force, just as the moon is in its matchless potency during a full moon, bright and unavoidable with its emotional pull. Then there are points when our grief is lurking in the shadows, lying in wait for our next emotional trigger. At times, we may even be unaware of it. We may have even temporarily forgotten it exists at all, with it having been totally eclipsed by our present moment.

I used to think that grief had a destination as when my mom died—that once I reached that mystical place I would stop grieving and I would be free. My grief would simply run its course like a bad cold. Thankfully, with time, our grief does temper. The authority with which it once controlled and consumed us seems to eventually subside and recede into the underbrush once again. But although it is transformed, it is never gone.

Please remember this, dear one: Just like the passing phases of the moon, your relationship to your grief over time will shift and change. Your grief is as unique as each star in the sky, and part of being fully human on this starship called Earth. Know that we shine together under the Widow's Moon, ever reaching towards the daybreak of our souls.

*I invite you to use the tools in the next section throughout your own moon phases of grief.*

# WIDOW'S LUNAR TOOLKIT

Throughout the moon cycles of grief, lunar medicine paves the way for nurturing and healing practices. As we move through our grief, the tools we use can have encouraging and far-reaching impacts. Learning to grieve well allows glimmers of hope to radiate through the darkness.

I know how totally overwhelming it can be when you first lose your loved one. Your world as you once knew it has been completely and permanently shifted. In some cases, it can feel like your heart has been irrevocably torn apart. You may feel frozen or have brain fog at the precise moment when a multitude of decisions is required. Chances are that making the time to take care of yourself may not be at the top of your to-do list.

It can feel daunting to even consider self-care when many other things are demanding your attention. But when you are ready, self-care should be number one on your list. Without it, you will not have the strength to carry on with all that lies in front of you. This grieving process may take you to places that will test your stamina and your endurance. You will need all of your reserves to handle the long haul. Taking care of yourself helps clear the fog and puts you in a better position to take care of others.

Please consider yourself and honor all that you are undertaking as you traverse this transformative path.

On the surface, it may not seem that this would be a fertile time of unlimited potential for spiritual and personal growth. Yet I have found that it can be just that. It takes time, compassion, courage, strength, determination, patience, and perseverance to keep moving through the emotional quagmire of grief. There is no destination and no timetable for completion. Devotion to your healing process can lead you to a higher awareness of who you are beyond your pain.

Take one day at a time, one breath at a time, and be loving and gentle with yourself. Remember that "this too shall pass." If you are not ready for any of this right now, simply put it aside until you are. One day, your orientation towards your grief will change. It may never completely go away, but you will develop a new relationship with it as time passes. This is all part of the natural evolution of grief. Allow its gifts to inform the *new* you that is evolving through this experience.

I have arranged these tools *loosely* based on three of the eight moon phases. Any of these tools can be interwoven as you cycle through your various stages of grief.

***Dark Moon or Balsamic Moon*** *is the darkest phase before the New Moon. As we grieve, this influence could last days, months, or years.*

*As we orbit this new world of grief, the dark moon is our portal for entering the sacred time of introspection, transition, nurturing, and surrender. It enables us to release that which no longer serves us and let go of the past, all in the service of regeneration and healing.*

## *You Don't Have to do this Alone*

You may find yourself needing to reach out for support during this darkest night. We expect that friends and family would be the first line of defense, but the truth is that sometimes they can't show up for you in the ways you might have assumed. Be open to receiving the help you need in expected and unexpected ways.

Keep in mind, too, that it can be difficult for others to know how to help. This may even keep people away since they feel inadequate and are afraid to ask or say the "wrong" thing. Because of this, it's important to be as specific as possible when you request support, filling in the blanks for them. I know this is a tough one for many of us who are grieving. The tendency is to isolate ourselves, not wanting to be a burden to others. But I encourage you to reach out if you feel you can.

## *Seek Help from Professionals*

You absolutely need a safe place to process your grief. Some of the most invaluable support can come through working with grief counselors, therapists, and holistic practitioners. Often, they can be more fully present with the entirety of your emotions. The aftermath of suicide requires another layer of reinforcement and healing. You don't have to suffer in silence; there are many loving people who have dedicated their lives to supporting others as they move through their grief and trauma.

## *Allow Your Emotions to Flow*

Allowing your emotions to flow through you is essential. You may want to cry, scream, or howl at the moon. You may feel numb or want to crawl under the covers. Maybe all of the above and then some! Simply sit with those emotions, free of judgment. Give them full permission to take their course, knowing they need the space to be seen, held, and heard.

My feelings were so intense and deep that I often feared that I'd get entangled or lost in a maze of grief. Thankfully, I learned over time that my emotions were circular and transitory in nature.

You may experience your grief in cycles or waves. You may have a good day or a good week and then get hit hard with another round when you least expect it. During those times, remember to wrap your arms around yourself, loving all of who you are in that moment. Ride it out if you can, trusting that your grief will take you to a place of healing.

## Prayer and Seeking Spiritual Support

Depending on your spiritual preferences or beliefs, you may want to use prayer or call in help and guidance from God, The Universe, Spirit, your angels, your guides, or your loved ones who have passed. Whatever terminology you feel comfortable with, remember that you are never alone and that you are always unconditionally loved beyond what you can imagine.

## Essential Oils

Essential oils are the extracted essences of various aromatic plants. They can be a wonderful addition to each one of your grief cycles, assisting with emotional balance and clearing the energy fields around your body or your living space. To begin with, I would suggest using them in a diffuser or mixed with spring water in a small cobalt blue glass spritzer bottle. For topical applications, they can be mixed with a carrier oil such as jojoba or fractionated coconut oil.

Soothing oils for grief include rose, lavender, geranium, roman chamomile, frankincense, cedarwood, sandalwood, patchouli, and vetiver.

Uplifting oils include jasmine, ylang ylang, peppermint, and all the citrus oils such as bergamot, neroli, grapefruit, lime, and orange.

In addition to essential oils, flowers themselves can light up your living space with their healing energy, helping to brighten your mood. Simply adding them to your grocery shopping cart each time you go to the store can be a self-loving and nurturing gesture.

### Nurture with Quiet Time and Quiet Space

There are numerous ways to nurture yourself during this moon cycle. If you like hot baths, regularly carving out *tub time* can be an opportunity to put the world on hold, be still, and be quiet. As part of your bath ritual, you can play meditative music, light candles, burn incense, use Epsom salts, or use soothing essential oils such as lavender to create the ultimate inner sanctum.

If it feels unattainable to carve out some extended undisturbed time, do something as simple as taking five minutes to stop everything. Stop moving, stop your mind, close your eyes, go within, and breathe. Just BE for those five minutes. After you have mastered that, congratulate and love yourself up. This is a great start. Maybe you could build on that, increasing to maybe ten minutes, or more gradually incorporating stillness into your daily schedule as time goes on.

The simple act of making a pot of soothing herbal tea can become a daily ritual to help you slow down and take a breath.

In addition, you may want to create a small spot or corner in your home that is just for YOU. For example, create an altar with things that are meaningful to you, including flowers, stones, crystals, pictures of angels, and anything else that feels inspirational and supportive.

Just like your time in the tub, this is your space to nurture and listen to your inner voice and *remember that you are more than your grief.* This could also be a time to release or surrender all the emotions that you have been holding throughout your day. This sacred place can be used for meditation, reading some inspirational words, journaling, crying, burning sage or incense, or using essential oils.

Regular massages, healings, or counseling sessions are other ways to cultivate nurturing support if at all feasible.

## *Nourish*

Be sure to include things that will nourish your body and soul. Remember, you deserve it, especially now! Sleeping and eating healthy foods are vitally important. When we are caught in our pain and anguish, it can feel like a huge effort to prepare nourishing food. We can find ourselves binge eating or not eating at all. If you can find a strategy to eat well at least some of the time, you will feel better overall and develop greater strength and resilience to manage all that lies before you. Please remember to hydrate with plenty of water! You may find it helpful to fill a large glass container each morning to keep out on the kitchen counter or take with you as a reminder to keep refilling your glass throughout the day.

## *Breathe*

When we are grieving, it's common for us to feel pressure in our heart center, making it difficult to breathe, especially while we are in high-stress fight-or-flight mode. It's important to remind ourselves to take deep expansive breaths. Our nervous system is taxed to the max during these emotionally intense times.

## *Meditation*

There are many types of meditation. If you already have a practice, but have put it on hold to grieve, this would be an opportune time to plug back into that. During your phases of grief, you may find it helpful to surrender your heart and soul to guided meditations. One app that offers many soothing and healing practices is "Insight Timer."

I have found this visualization to be beneficial:

*Place your awareness on your heart center, that tender place that feels or felt so broken. Softly and gently hold your hand over your heart. This automatically brings your attention and awareness to that part of your physical body. Breathe in as deeply as you can. Now, imagine a beam of divine love streaming through your hands into your heart. Imagine this light from the Divine filling your heart with love and soothing your emotions with each breath.*

*Your breath will become fuller through this process. Stay with this as long as it feels comforting. Now turn your attention to the rest of your body. You may feel a tightness in your solar plexus just below your heart center. Continue on to this area, positioning your hand over your stomach and bringing your attention and breath there until you feel a release and calm.*

This can be repeated in any part of your body as needed. With the Universal healing energy streaming through your hands, you may feel a sense of peace as you continue with this technique. This exercise helped me to be more present and calmed my nervous system, alleviating moments of overwhelm.

So, let's be mindful of our sacred stillness and breath, and allow ourselves to be breathed by the Universal Force that we are all an integral part of. This is a new habit that takes practice and time to create. I've found that it is well worth the effort.

## *Grounding*

Along with breath awareness, making sure we are grounded is an essential component to helping us feel more focused, relaxed, and safe.

*Begin by imagining that there is a beam of golden light or a root at the base of your spine, your root chakra. From that place, imagine this light streaming deep down into the center of the earth attaching to your own designated spot, created just for you. When you connect to this magical site, you are securely grounded and held in love and light. You can also access the healing energy of our Mother Earth by drawing that in through this same channel or grounding cord, bringing it up through your feet, legs, and throughout your body. She is always there willing to help if we ask.*

The essential oils of frankincense, vetiver, cedarwood, sandalwood, and patchouli are thought to be helpful for grounding.

### Nature

Spending time in nature on a daily basis is vital for us. If you don't have access to open space, maybe you have a park nearby, a backyard, a patio, or a deck. Sitting there feeds the soul, helping you feel more aligned with your spiritual, emotional, and physical bodies. While out, be aware of your surroundings, the sounds, the wind, and the sky. Feel your feet on the ground. All of nature is here for us to access and honor. It can give a much-needed respite so that you can process all that you are carrying and allow insights to surface.

We don't want to overlook the healing spirits of the plant kingdom. If you go on walks regularly, you may see a tree or trees that you feel drawn to. These trees are your helpers along this path. Go to them, cry with them, and ask them to ground all your fears, pain, and suffering through their roots down into Mother Earth, where she can absorb and assimilate, using those emotions as compost. Ask them to help you feel grounded when you feel like you are spinning out of control. Be sure to express your love and gratitude each time.

### Movement

Moving our bodies can also help us ground and release. Walking, hiking, running, biking, yoga, qi gong, and tai chi are just a few things you can try on your own or with an online or in-person class. Remember to take it slow if you are just starting out.

The curative tonic of music and dance inspires your channels of pain or even joy to open! If you are in the car, crank up the music and sing your heart out. That feels great too. The key is to allow all those trapped emotions to start flowing.

*The **New Moon** begins a new cycle. It is a time for planting seeds of intention for moving forward. Invite the magic of manifestation into your life. In your grieving cycle, you may be feeling a sense of renewal after your season in the darkness.*

## Permission

The New Moon has its distinctive pull, drawing you into its orbit as you journey into your own personal world of grief. Only you can give yourself permission to form a crack through the darkness, allowing your inner light to shine through. Only you can choose to heal, love, and live, finding your True Self while creating a meaningful life. This is the greatest gift of the New Moon.

Now that we are ready to transition into the New Moon phase, we are better equipped to usher in the light of our hopes and dreams into our physical reality.

## Affirmations

Using affirmations in this phase can raise your vibration, which will support and elevate your emotions. This reinforces your superpower as the co-creator of your life. *Remember to not only visualize as you speak the words but really feel into what you are saying as if it's already happening. In other words, feel it in your bones. Feel how grateful you are for this gift.*

There are affirmations between the chapters of this book. Feel free to use any that resonate with you. You can also create your own. Simply fill in the blank with what you feel is important for you. The possibilities are endless.

Try writing your affirmations on Post-it notes. Placed around the house, they can serve as helpful reminders. Put them on mirrors where you can look yourself in the eyes and speak the words out loud, which only adds to the powerful results. While you are doing this, you may want to try the simple action of smiling. My wise brother, Bill, taught me that trick and it really helps to shift your energy.

## *Journaling*

Journaling is therapeutic for releasing any unexpressed feelings, practicing gratitude, and getting clear on your next step. Let your words reveal that which resides in your heart and soul. You will feel lighter and know that your voice has been heard.

You can also create a ritual around journaling. Asking for spiritual guidance as you write can further assist you in developing clarity on what you want to manifest in your life.

To set the stage, light a candle, put on some soothing music, and sit quietly before you start. First, anchor and ground yourself into the present moment. Then, let the words flow.

In this New Moon phase, you can use journaling as a tool to begin dreaming your new life into existence. Journaling prompts include:

How do I want my life to feel?

Who am I now?

How do I see myself evolving?

What is my purpose now?

What gifts can I offer to the world?

How can I best support my path now?

How can I best love myself right now?

You may want to write daily love notes to yourself. You could do that in your journal, or you could find a beautiful container and colored paper. Cut up the paper into small pieces so that they are ready to go. Each morning or night (or both), remember to honor and love yourself. You deserve it!

I have included journaling in the New Moon phase, but it's also an invaluable practice to use during the Dark Moon phase to allow another outlet for your emotions to be felt and heard.

*Full Moon is your most powerful crowning moment—a time to shine brightly, basking in the light that you have been cultivating in the previous phases. Rest in gratitude for the inner work, spiritual guidance, and support that has brought you to this moment. This is a time when you can let your creativity bloom and release all that is no longer serving your soul's highest good.*

## Moon Bathing

Have you ever noticed how good it feels to gaze at the moon, spurring our connection with the eternal nature of the cosmos? Moon bathing is an ancient practice of basking in the sacredness of the moon's natural luminescence. This potent light infusion can be done at any one of the moon phases but is most advantageous during a full moon. The feminine nature of the moon can assist us with recharging our depleted energy levels and balancing our emotions. Take a walk, grab a chair, or just lay on the earth and spend some time under the moon and stars taking in that nourishing lunar magic.

## *Moon Bathing for your Crystals or Stones*

If you have any stones or crystals that you have chosen to work with, this is an opportune time to cleanse and recharge them energetically in the moonlight. Since they can accumulate and absorb various energies, it is a great idea to make this a regular practice. Simply wash them and place them outside on a natural surface. If possible, leave them out for 24 hours. Be aware of those that are sun or water sensitive. For example, selenite is damaged in water.

## *Moon Water*

The moon can supercharge your water with its mystical lifeforce. Simply fill a large mason jar with purified or spring water and let it sit under the moonlight until morning. You can drink this water or fill a small spray bottle, adding essential oils to cleanse your aura or living space.

## *Creativity*

As you move further along through your grief, you may feel inspired to access your creativity. Remember, we are all creators. When we tap into the field of creativity and eventually see the results of our efforts, we are reminded that we have the power to co-create a new path in our lives. The possibilities are endless. Contrary to popular belief, you don't need to have any special artistic abilities to do this. Photography, painting, drawing, writing, collage, gardening, sewing, and knitting are all ways to process your emotions and cultivate your inner joy.

## *Japanese Kintsugi Ceremony*

Kintsugi is the Japanese practice of putting broken ceramic pieces back together with gold. The premise is that by embracing our own 'brokenness,' we are able to re-define and celebrate who we have become in this new form. With the potency of the full moon, we can highlight this awakening as an art of 'becoming' and re-birth with a Kintsugi Ceremony. (Please see my resource section for kits you can buy).

## Practicing Gratitude

Believe it or not, there is a place to include gratitude in our grieving process. While we are caught in the grips of despair, it may seem impossible or unimaginable to find anything to feel grateful for. However, when we make room for gratitude, we can help to shift our awareness in times of extreme pain and hopelessness.

I am not saying that you should use gratitude to deny your emotions or to make it all go away with positive thinking. But it can help you change the channel even if it is just for one moment. Sometimes we can really use those momentary breathers while we are grieving.

You may want to create a daily gratitude journal to remind yourself of those things and people who are blessing you with their presence. Your creativity could spill onto those pages with colored pencils or markers. There is always a light shining if we are open to receiving its warm and eternal wisdom. There are many gifts still surrounding us and many to be discovered. I invite you to give gratitude a chance by incorporating it into your life.

## Forgiveness

Another ritual that you can use is the ancient Hawaiian Ho'oponopono prayer of forgiveness. It can help you heal the deep heart wounds from your past or present, whether it be forgiving yourself, others, or even your grief. You can use this at your altar, on your walks in nature or as you are going about your day. The main intention is to invoke repentance, forgiveness, gratitude, and love.

Simply repeat these words:

I am sorry.

Forgive me.

Thank you.

I love you.

As you choose to incorporate this into your life you may want to try journaling about it, making note of any internal or external shifts you are having in response to this practice. For example, you may feel more empowered or more at peace.

### Writing Letters to Yourself and Your Lost Loved One

I wrote many letters to Claude in my journal. Some were filled with love, some with anger, and some with forgiveness and acceptance. I found that this gave me the opportunity to express things that I needed to say to him. My feelings and thoughts had a place to land and be heard. Yours could be love letters, letters filled with anger, or both. Either way, this can give those feelings a place to rest, thus bringing great peace, calm, and healing.

The Full Moon is the most opportune time to release those deep emotions and anything you want to leave behind.

Take the letters of anger, forgiveness, or any emotions you want to express or leave behind and do a Full Moon ceremony. Just like your *altar time,* you can create a sacred space by lighting a candle, smudging, or using essential oils—whatever you choose.

Next, you may choose to burn those letters, releasing that energy up to Spirit to be transmuted so that you can move forward with a clean slate. *Please be sure to use a fire-safe container.* As you watch the flames, say your prayers and affirmations. Examples include: *I am ready to leave the past behind. I forgive myself and my lost loved one. I trust my inner guidance system.* Use your creativity to add to this list.

Afterward, you may want to dance under the moon, literally or figuratively. You have come so far on this journey through grief. You can celebrate all that you have released and all that is no longer serving you. You are ready to embrace joy and freedom after this long journey home to your Self.

*I embrace Joy!*
*I embrace Freedom!*
*I love myself enough to do this!*

# RESOURCES

*Healing Practitioners*
Eeris Kallil
Licensed Massage Therapist
https://www.bodyworkwisdom.com
www.boulderoncologymassage.com

Gwen Cupples
Spiritual Teacher, Master Hypnotherapist, Energy Healer, Sound Healer, Intuitive Guide
and Life Coach
https://www.sourcesong.com

Lisa Bluedeer
Shamanic Practitioner, Intuitive Healer
https://www.bluedeershamanichealing.com/

Lisa Schiavone
Teacher and Practitioner of Hypno-Journey, Reiki, Archetypal and Evolutionary Astrology
https://lisaschiavone.com
http://hypno-journey.com/

Marianne Lindstrom Mitchell
Energy Healer and Spiritual Counselor
http://appalachianpriestess.com

Mark Graycar Chiropractic
Non-Force Chiropractor in Boulder, CO
https://www.graycarchiro.com

**Coaches**
Bryna Haynes
Founder & CEO of WorldChangers Media
www.worldchangers.media

Johanna Walker
Speaking Coach, Storytelling Expert and TEDx speaker
https://www.johannawalker.com

Skye Zimmerman
Coaching and Transformational Healing
https://www.skyevizioncoaching.com

**Grief Support**

Be sure to look into your local hospice centers and churches. Many offer free or low cost grief support.

If you are on social media, Facebook and Instagram have many groups and pages for inspiration and grief support.

Beth Erlander, Grief Friend
Creative Arts Psychotherapist and Grief Support Practitioner, MA, LPC, ATR
https://betherlander.com/

Grief Support Network

- Mindful Grieving Yoga Therapy Programs
- Mindful Connections for High School Students
- Mindful Connections for Middle School Students
- Mindful Parenting Classes
- Community Circles
- Network of Providers
- Community Resources
https://griefsupportnet.org
Email: info@griefsupportnet.org

Center for Somatic Grieving

- Mindful Grieving 200 hour Yoga Therapy Teacher Training Program
- Awakening Through Grief Wellness Retreats
- Professional training programs for somatic, mindfulness-based grief support
- Workshops, Immersions, Podcasts, Talks and Mentorships
  Email: wendy@centerforsomaticgrieving.com
  www.griefsupportnet.org

The Living and Dying Consciously Project
https://www.livinganddyingconsciouslyproject.org

Susannah Conway
https://www.susannahconway.com/

***Courses for Romantic Love***
Arielle Ford and Claire Zammit
Love Codes
https://evolvingwisdom.com/fp/global/lovecodes/enroll/c/

Matt Boggs
https://www.bravethinkinginstitute.com/faculty/mathew-boggs

*Books and Courses for Personal and Spiritual Growth*

Kris Carr
*Kris shares an abundance of valuable tools in many categories for living and nurturing your well-being, including self-care tips, meditations, courses, healthy diet recommendations, The Results Journal, Crazy Sexy Love Notes, Inner Circle Wellness, and much more. She is a dose of sunshine!*
https://kriscarr.com/

Hay House
*Started by the late Louise Hay, this site has an abundance of books, meditations, and courses relating to your personal and spiritual growth.*
https://www.hayhouse.com

The Shift Network
Transformational Education and Media
https://theshiftnetwork.com

Sacred Science
Shamanism, Herbalism, and Energy Medicine
https://www.thesacredscience.com/sacred-shop/#allproductslink

Paul Selig
*I Am the Word*, Tarcher/Penguin, 2010
*The Book of Love and Creation*, Tarcher/Penguin, 2012
To see a list of his other books and courses go to:
https://paulselig.com

Elizabeth Wilcock
*Priestess Path Lineages of Light*
http://www.ElizabethWilcock.com

Joe Dispenza
*Breaking the Habit of Being Yourself*, Hay House, 2012
*Becoming Supernatural*, Hay House, 2017
https://drjoedispenza.com

Mike Dooley
*Notes from the Universe and various books and courses about spirituality and manifestation.*
https://www.tut.com

### *Spiritual and Ceremonial Products*

Angel Cards
Kathy Tyler and Joy Drake

Crazy Sexy Love Notes
Kris Carr

Life Honey (Kintsugi Ceremony Kits)
https://lifehoney.com/pages/about

Medicine Cards
Jamie Sams and David Carson

Rebecca's Herbal Apothecary
*Various herbal remedies, body, and aromatherapy products.*
https://www.rebeccasherbs.com

Shamans Market
*Various ceremonial products to help you create your sacred space.*
https://www.shamansmarket.com/

### Digital Meditations

Insight Timer
https://insighttimer.com

Calm
https://www.calm.com

### Soothing Music Artists

Anugama
Aeolia
Dean Evenson
Deuter
Hilary Stagg
Liquid Mind
Snatam Kaur

### Health and Food

Irene Lyon
Smart Body Smart Mind and Nervous System Rewire
https://irenelyon.com/

Food Matters
https://www.foodmatters.com

Food Revolution Network
https://foodrevolution.org

*Books on Grief, the Afterlife, and Inspiration*

Almstedt, Debbie Zylstra, *Zibu: The Power of Angelic Symbology*, Zibu Publishing, 2007

Andrews, Ted, *Animal Speak: The Spiritual & Magical Powers of Creatures Great and Small*, Llewellyn Publications, 2002

Angelee, Jennifer, *Beloved, I Can Show You Heaven: A True Story of Life After Death Communication Between Soulmates*, 2020

Austill-Clausen, Rebecca, *Change Maker: How My Brother's Death Woke Up My Life*, She Writes Press, 2016

Cassou, Michelle, and Stewart Cubley, *Life, Paint, and Passion*, Tarcher/Penguin, 1995

Conway, Susannah, *This I Know: Notes on Unraveling the Heart*, Skirt!, 2012

Dillard, Sherrie, *Sacred Signs & Symbols: Awaken to the Messages & Synchronicities That Surround You*, Llewellyn Publications, 2017

Foster, Jeff, *You Were Never Broken*, Sounds True, 2020. *The Way of Rest, Finding the Courage to Hold Everything in Love*, Sounds True, 2016

Hay, Louise, *You Can Heal Your Life*, Hay House, 1984. *Mirror Work*, Louise Hay, 2016

Jackson, Laura Lynne, *Signs: The Secret Language of the Universe*, Random House, 2020

Kagan, Annie, *The Afterlife of Billy Fingers: How My Bad-Boy Brother Proved to Me There's Life After Death*, Hampton Roads Publishing, 2013

Kubler-Ross, Elisabeth, and David Kessler, *Life Lessons: Two Experts on Death and Dying Teach Us About the Mysteries of Life and Living*, Scribner, 2003

Licata, Matt, *That Path Is Everywhere: Uncovering the Jewels Hidden Within You*, Wandering Yogi Press, 2017. *A Healing Space: Befriending Ourselves in Difficult Times*, Sounds True, 2020

Malchiodi, Cathy A., *The Soul's Palette*, Shambhala Publications, 2002

Pajevic, Tanja, *The Secret Life of Grief*, Abbondanza Press, 2016

Pueblo, Yung, *Inward*, Andrews McNeal Publishing, 2018

Severson Kasmirski, Risë, *When Paradise Speaks: A Remarkable, True Story of Friendship, After Death Communication and Art Heals*, Lovitude Publishing, 2020

Simmons, Robert, *The Book of Stones, Revised Edition: Who They Are & What They Teach*, North Atlantic Books, 2015

Tarantino, Janet D., *Dying to See, Revelations About God, Jesus, Our Pathways, and the Nature of the Soul*, Day Agency Publishing, 2020

Zuba, Tom, *Permission to Mourn: A New Way to Do Grief*, Bish Press, 2014

# ACKNOWLEDGMENTS

It's hard for me to ignore the synchronicities marking this, the 9th year since Claude's suicide. Ending with an 18th chapter also links up with the number 9. In numerology, you would typically add the numbers 1+8=9. Nine is a number of completion and initiation, defining the final phase of my Widow's Moon cycle. This book has been my baby—in development and gestation during those nine years, just as I have been.

Looking back, I see that this is a time like no other to birth this project into the world. Unknowingly, all my stops and starts have led me to this moment of divine perfection.

My deepest gratitude to those in the seen and unseen realms who continue to support and love me as I move through this mysterious experience we call life. Those in the unseen world include Claude and my angelic assistants, who have been infinitely patient and persistent with me through all my fears and resistance. They have consistently reassured me that writing this book is an important part of my soul's purpose. Without their consistent words of wisdom, this book would not be in your hands right now.

These spiritual helpers have sent many in the physical world to assist and prepare me for this pursuit. My sister, Terra Lynn Joy, shares the same birthday (ten years apart), and as a fellow writer she has been my number one supporter, always believing in the tiniest sprout of the possibility that I could actually write a book and ceaselessly saying "YES, you can do this." My brother, Bill Clark, has also provided unwavering optimism and love.

Marianne Mitchell Lindstrom, Gwen Cupples, Eeris Kallil, Lisa Schiavone, and Mark Graycar, you have been among the many healers, teachers, and dear friends acting as surrogate 'midwives' who have held sacred space for me. You've helped me put the pieces of my body, mind, and spirit together when I wondered if that were even possible, always encouraging me to love myself, remember the truth of my divinity, and continue listening to my inner knowing. Your support has enabled me to trust and believe in that initial vision, that seed of consciousness of what lay ahead.

It wouldn't be fair to leave out the most significant teacher of all: *grief.* I never would have imagined years ago that I could celebrate the transformational journey you have taken me on. Yet here I am. After the many years of pain, suffering, and healing I am grateful to have found the light within and to share my discoveries with others who are still searching.

Linny Sweet, my fellow widow on this transformational path, thank you for your friendship and love, and for always reassuring me that my words are healing and will be helpful to others.

Bryna Haynes got me started four years ago with her online book writing course. Back then I was still stuck in the "who am I to write this book?" mentality. My confidence at that point was low (to say the least). Despite that, I always remember her saying "you are exactly where you are meant to be." I held on to those words. Thank you, Bryna.

Another gift from Bryna was her introduction to Rebecca van Laer, my editor and my trusty guardian keeper of this manuscript, who gently steered this ship to help me craft and deliver my book to a place beyond my wildest expectations.

Johanna Walker's speaking course ignited my passion to delve deeper into my story, which in turn influenced how it was expressed and articulated in this book. Ultimately, she reinforced that I have an important story to tell.

Geoff Affleck has shepherded me through this otherwise overwhelming publishing process with his calm reassuring attitude and proficiency. His team has helped me bring my dream into a stunning visual reality.

Steve Gaudin, thank you for your friendship and for helping me relax enough to get the fabulous photos to use for this book and my website.

Noah, my dearest son, has in his own way supported me through my many meltdowns over this past year as I fervently worked on this book. When I sometimes felt like I would come unglued, he never let me down, continually bolstering my spirits. His editorial prowess was greatly appreciated as he painstakingly read and reread along with me as I worked out all the kinks.

My deepest gratitude to all of my dedicated beta readers and the supporters who have endorsed *Widow's Moon*. Thank you for devoting your precious time to reading my manuscript and for lending your valuable feedback and encouragement.

Claude's mom, Eleanor, championed me to finish this book and loved every word of my first draft. I had hoped she would be able to read my completed memoir, but sadly, she passed away before she could. On the day she died, I heard this inspirational message from her spirit that I think we all could benefit from reading.

> *So now for the good stuff, my dear. This Universe is full of love and light as you already know. What you have not yet discovered is that you are the center of your own Universe. You have the power and the ability to co-create. Please do know this is the TRUTH! You have heard this, but you have not let it sink in and let it be an aspect of the way you're living your daily life. I want you to REALLY HEAR THIS! You can and do have the POWER to create ALL that exists in your life! FEEL IT! KNOW IT!*

*NOW! I did not understand this when I was embodied. But now I am free to experience even more unlimited gifts and I want you to have this awareness NOW. You can be at PEACE just as I have been infusing you with all afternoon. Just let it happen. Let the LOVE in! It's a vibration. Can you feel it? It's a frequency of LOVE. Not romantic love with all its attachments. This is altogether different. It's a ONENESS LOVE.*

Thank you, Eleanor!

I thank my dearest beloved, Claude. You reached for my hand on our first date, telling me you would lift me up the mountain with your faith and belief in me, helping me move beyond my limiting programs and self-talk. Twenty-seven years ago, you saw my strengths and potential, the woman I have evolved into now. It took me all these years and with grief as my greatest teacher to land me at the top of the mountain. One way or another, you helped me get there. Thank you for your endless love and for seeing in me what I wasn't ready to see. I will carry that in my heart always and until we meet again.

Finally, I bow down to *you*, dear reader. I wrote this for you as much as for myself, and I am truly grateful and feel honored that you have chosen *Widow's Moon* to be part of your own journey to healing and wholeness.

# ABOUT THE AUTHOR

Cara Hope Clark was born into the world during a full lunar eclipse in Providence, Rhode Island. At a young age, she knew she was more sensitive than most, and has always felt drawn to the mystical realm. As she grew into adulthood in her twenties, she began to find her way to various healing practitioners who would guide her to discovering her life purpose. Her calling to help others in the healing arts led her to Santa Fe, New Mexico, where she received training in massage therapy, Reiki, and energy work.

In 1989, she moved to San Francisco and studied at the Academy of Intuition Medicine in Mill Valley, California. She had a private practice for fifteen years as a massage therapist and intuitive energy healer before becoming a full-time mom in 1998. She has been devoted to personal and spiritual growth for over forty years.

Cara holds a Bachelor of Fine Arts degree from the University of Rhode Island. As her son grew older, her interest in the visual arts eventually brought her to creating a body of work of abstract paintings.

These paintings reflected a connection to Spirit that allowed healing energy to flow onto the canvas.

Her husband's suicide in 2012 brought her to yet another calling—sharing her story of grief and transformation by writing this book. Widow's Moon has been another form of creative expression including energy transmissions from the Divine.

She currently calls Boulder, Colorado her home, together with her son, Noah, and their beloved dog, Lyra. Photography, writing, painting, gardening, cooking, music, spending time with loved ones, and being out in nature give her joy and solace.

If you would like to learn more or contact Cara, please reach out to widowsmoon.com or email her at carahope@carahopeclark.com.

# EXPAND THE LOVE

Thank you for journeying through the pages of Widow's Moon. It's my deepest hope that you have benefited from reading and found the support you need. If you feel that others will find it helpful, please take a moment and go to the site where you purchased your book and rate your experience to get the word out. This will help me share my voice with more readers like you.

With love and gratitude,

Cara Hope

CPSIA information can be obtained
at www.ICGtesting.com
Printed in the USA
BVHW030158080921
616296BV00005B/211